A FIGHTING SPIRIT

Ashoka Gupta, January 2008

A FIGHTING SPIRIT

Selected Writings of
Ashoka Gupta

Introduction by
Jasodhara Bagchi

Compiled and Edited by
Sarmistha Dutta Gupta
Narayani Gupta

NIYOGI
BOOKS

Published by
NIYOGI BOOKS
D-78, Okhla Industrial Area, Phase-I
New Delhi-110 020, India
Tel: 91-11-26816301, 49327000
Fax: 91-11-26810483, 26813830
email: niyogibooks@gmail.com
www.niyogibooks.com

Edited by Sarmistha Dutta Gupta and Narayani Gupta

Design: Write Media

ISBN: 978-93-81523-65-0
Year of Publication: 2013

Printed at: Niyogi Offset Pvt. Ltd., New Delhi, India

Contents

Stepping out into the world

Acknowledgements

Ashoka Gupta spoke vividly and fluently in Bangla, English and Hindi, and wrote rapidly and with great ease in the first two languages. She wrote two books—*Noakhalir Durjoger Din* in Bangla (published by Naya Udyog in 1999) and *In the Path of Service* in English (published by Stree in 2005). This was drawn from her reminiscences, dictated to Sipra Bhattacharya and Ranjana Dasgupta, who then painstakingly translated it into English.

But there was much more that she wrote and there are a number of radio-talks where she spoke. This book puts together some of her other writings, most of it originally written in Bangla, to mark the centenary of her birth. This collection became possible because of Sarmistha Dutta Gupta who did the content selection and identified the translators. About the selection, she said, 'If I hadn't known Ashoka-di personally and hadn't researched on women in late colonial Bengal with Ashoka-di generously guiding me from time to time, I couldn't have put this together.' She in turn was able to do so because, in the course of two years after her passing, Ashoka Gupta's papers and letters had been meticulously catalogued and listed by an archivist. It is only because of Tapan Khan, who undertook this task with the time he could spare from his work, that we have an archive of Ashoka Gupta's papers that should soon find its place in a larger repository.

Our grateful thanks to the translators—Sayantan Dasgupta, Somak Ghoshal, Sutanuka Ghosh and Vikram Iyengar. We thank Mandira Sen for readily giving permission to include an essay published in *The Trauma and the Triumph* (Stree, 2003). Kenneth Gustafson took photographs of Ashoka Gupta in her last years, and we are privileged to publish them. The library of the All India Women's Conference in Delhi has an excellent collection of photographs, and we are beholden to the President, the Librarian and Dr Aparna Basu for their kindness in letting us include eleven of them. Jasodhara Bagchi, who had a close association with Ashoka Gupta, was unquestionably the most appropriate person to write the 'Introduction' to this book. We express our gratitude to her. What has made this book possible in an amazingly short time is the generous and cheerful help of Tultul and Bikash Niyogi and of Supriya Mukherjee, and what has made it such an attractive one was the painstaking care of Ritu and Navkala of Write Media, who indulged all our demands, down to having Ashoka Gupta's spinning-wheel serve as a section-divider.

July 8, 2008

Preface

The afternoon of July 8, 2008—the day she left us...an empty chair, a long bell-cord, two tables piled with books and papers, clips, a stapler, a clip-board, and a cordless phone. A young woman came in smiling, asking for *Mashima*, explaining that she had come all the way from her village by train to see her, a four-hour journey. She refused to believe what we told her and went into the inner room to look for *Mashima*...

It took us all a long time to get used to the empty chair. When you went up the steps to 404/5 Gariahat Road in Kolkata, Ashoka Gupta would be sitting in her low-slung chair facing the door; if you went into the inner room, she would be at the head of the dining table. Her smile greeted every visitor. She was available for everyone, for every phone-call, from 8 in the morning till 10 at night. At 95 years of age, she had the energy of a 21-year-old and the enthusiasm of a child for whom every day held new delights. Absorption in work was her way of conquering the loneliness she suffered after the passing of her husband in 1989 and the terrible grief of the loss of her son Partha Sarathi in 1999 and her daughter Shakuntala in 2003.

There were traces of her work everywhere—in every room there were cupboards and makeshift shelves stuffed with papers.

We, bewildered, began by piling all the books, papers and tapes in one room. One person who could have made sense of it all was Shakuntala (Kunta), her eldest daughter, who lived in Kolkata. For two decades, quietly and competently, she had been her unofficial secretary, and had inherited the mantle of the Girl Guides movement—and made time for this in the interstices of teaching and research, and the shared responsibilities of a joint family. But Kunta had left this world, quietly and without fuss, five years earlier. In her absence, the work was being done by Krishna, the housekeeper, and Singeswar, Ashoka Gupta's Man Friday. Singeswar could read Hindi, Bangla and English, and not only was totally devoted to her but had acquired some of her encyclopaedic memory. And then came the wonder-worker—in the form of Tapan Khan, who brought order into the chaos, and sat day after day, month after month, working every minute with silent concentration, sorting it all.

It was not easy—official reports were interleaved with restaurant menus and scribbled phone numbers, letters were not in any order with bundles stuffed into shoeboxes or ragged handbags, Christmas cards were separated from their respective envelopes which made it impossible to identify the senders, and photographs had no indication of where and when they were taken...However, this was not the disorder of an indolent person, but of someone who had so many irons in the fire that she did not allow herself time to take a break between different activities, and moved breathlessly from one to the next. And it did not matter as long as she was alive—she knew exactly where everything was, no matter how randomly placed—the colour of the file, the shelf where it had been put. She did not use a computer because she did not need one—she was as good as a computer herself. She had explained why she had such a vivid memory—it was because every day for her was full of meaning and purpose. As Gopal Gandhi said: 'For Ashoka-di, there was no pausing between activities. It was an incessant commitment to the service of the people'.

It was not just her own papers she had stashed away. The papers of her husband, Saibal Kumar Gupta, and of her mother Jyotirmoyee Debi, had also been meticulously collected. She had been able to put together five books out of articles written by Saibal Kumar Gupta after he passed away in 1989, and handed over a large trunk of his letters and notes to the Nehru Memorial Library in New Delhi.

That Jyotirmoyee Debi came to be recognised as one of the most original and productive of women writers in Bengal was due to her two daughters—Anjali Chatterjee, her youngest, who faithfully copied out her stories and sent them to journals for publication, and Ashoka, who worked to get them published as books. Later, in

The Gupta family in 1967. Clockwise from top: Saibal Gupta, Kajal, Shakuntala, Ashoka, Apala, Narayani, Partha Sarathi, Kasturi, little Srirupa

the 1990s, the dedicated efforts of Professor Jasodhara Bagchi led to their reincarnation in the impressive 5-volume *Jyotirmoyee Debir Rachana Sankalan*.

And the full measure of the person could not be learned only from her papers. She was a mother who wore khadi saris but bought a smart swimsuit for her daughter; a mother-in-law who always ordered in South Indian breakfasts on Sundays for her Malayali son-in-law. She was a woman who enjoyed wearing a white satin housecoat identical to that worn by her friend of decades 'Baby-*mashi*', 'so that people will mistake us for twins'; commanded her daughter-in-law to 'Haashao' ('Make me laugh'); remembered everyone's favourite dish; sent out for balloons on her 90th birthday when a 4-year-old guest complained that no birthday party was complete without balloons, and delighted in the company of her grandchildren and great grandchildren. She read a government report with the same absorption with which she read a novel or a children's storybook. She loved visiting places she had not seen, sampling food she had never eaten (even camel and horse meat!), enjoyed music, going to films and plays. When her taxi ground to a halt during a Kolkata monsoon and the water began to seep in, instead of going hysterical as any normal person on the road would have, she decided to enjoy the downpour and told her son to roll up his trousers and go buy some piping-hot samosas and jalebis for an impromptu picnic!

She defied every stereotype—of the earnest social worker, of the sophisticated wife of a senior bureaucrat, of the stately president of an all-India organisation. Her eyes twinkled with mischief as easily as they grew soft with sympathy, her voice could belt out an order as well as ignite hope in a distressed woman. Everyone who knew her had a personal story to relate, everyone felt he or she was special to her. The lines inscribed on the Statue of Liberty might equally have been said of her:

Give me your tired, your poor,
Your huddled masses yearning to breathe free

This was Ashoka, *Mez-di*, *Boudi*, Ashoka-di, Ma, Ashoka-*mashi*, *Jethima*, *Mamima*, *Pishi*, *Didima* and *Thamma*, *Boro-didima*...who lived every day as if it was a new adventure. *Carpe diem* was said for people like her. And wherever she is, we hope she will read this book, and smile over the photographs...

Narayani Gupta

on behalf of the family of Ashoka Gupta
Kasturi Gupta Menon, daughter
Apala Gupta Egan, daughter
Kajal Dasgupta, son-in-law
Srikandath Narayan Menon, son-in-law
John Robert Egan, son-in-law
Srirupa Dasgupta, granddaughter
Nilanjana Dasgupta, granddaughter
Himadri Shikhar Gupta, grandson
Raghubir Menon, grandson
Niharika Gupta, granddaughter
John William Gupta Egan, grandson
Conrad James Gupta Egan, grandson
Pablo Jenik, grandson-in-law
Lovleen Bhullar, granddaughter-in-law
Robi Jenik, great-grandson
Raka Jenik, great-granddaughter

Introduction

Jasodhara Bagchi

Ashoka Gupta was one of the rare fighting spirits, who made social service her calling. Born in 1912, she was the daughter of Jyotirmoyee Debi (later to become well-known as a writer) who belonged to an enlightened Bengali family in the employ of the Maharajas of Jaipur. Ashoka Gupta's life trajectory made her evolve into an unusual embodiment of a middle-class Bengali women's aspirations and achievements, coming out of the crucible of anti-colonial struggles and the enormous hardships that Indian men and women went through in the forties and fifties of the twentieth century.

Being a direct recipient of her unstinted warmth and affection, it is very difficult for me to take this somewhat distant view of her accomplishments, but this commemoration volume that marks her birth centenary does demand a certain kind of celebratory evaluation of her work's significance into which the generation that follows ours must be initiated.

Looking back on Ashoka Gupta's extraordinary life journey, one will have to begin with noting her probity, when she described her own memoir—entitled, very appropriately, *In the Path of Service*—as her memories of a 'changing century'.[1] When she passed away at the age of 95, she had lived through a century of cataclysmic change, seeing India win her freedom, as I have said elsewhere, 'in an idiom of loss'.[2] She achieved a true meshing of 'the home and the world' which brings to mind Wordsworth's Skylark: 'True to the kindred points of heaven

---

[1] Ashoka Gupta, *In the Path of Service: Memories of a Changing Century*, eds Sipra Bhattacharya and Ranjana Das Gupta (Kolkata: Stree, 2005), first reprint 2008.

[2] Jasodhara Bagchi, 'Freedom in an Idiom of Loss' in *The Trauma and the Triumph: Gender and Partition in Eastern India*, eds. Jasodhara Bagchi and Subharanjan Dasgupta (Stree: Kolkata, 2003).

Ashoka Sen, 1931, before her marriage. Ashoka took her matriculation examinations in 1930 and joined Bethune College to study Mathematics. In 1933, she was married to Saibal Kumar Gupta, an ICS officer, and had to leave for her marital home in Barisal in East Bengal. Unable to continue her honours course in Mathematics, she had to settle for a BSc degree. She did well, scoring the highest marks in Chemistry.

and home'! Her domestic life, both before and after marriage to the redoubtable khadi-clad ICS officer Saibal Gupta, forms an important parallel journey symbiotically related to her formidable public world of social work. The many hair-splitting debates which have occurred in feminist theorising on 'public-private' divide will no doubt find a challenging study in this remarkable account. It would, however, not do to simply rely on her own memoir. There are other things one will have to look at in order to place her in perspective. This book will certainly open up some of these other aspects.

Ashoka Gupta was an inheritor of the movement for women's emancipation and empowerment that was central to India's struggle for anti-colonial modernity. As an active member of the All India Women's Conference (AIWC), the first all-India women's organisation, formed in 1927, Ashoka Gupta both received from and contributed to the rapid change that came over the lives of our women. New lineaments of class subjectivity were becoming visible in the striking choices that Ashoka Gupta made and tried to make available to the generations to follow.

After she lost her father Kiron Chandra Sen, a promising lawyer in Patna, to an untimely death when she was just six, Ashoka's life went through a process of apparent unsettling that eventually contributed to her cosmopolitan personality. Abinash Chandra Sen took his widowed daughter Jyotirmoyee with her six children to his spacious home in Jaipur. However, the elder son Arun was sent away for schooling to Delhi to the house of Abinash Sen's younger brother. It was her remarkable mother Jyotirmoyee Debi who insisted that little Ashoka too should go to Delhi along with her brother, as the feudal set-up in Jaipur had few good schools. Eventually, she relocated to Kolkata and joined the Duff School—an experience she cherished because of the initiation into the Girl Guide movement of which she was to become a prominent all-India leader and which helped her to connect local issues with the international aspect of the movement. Later, she studied in St Margaret's Convent, where she began to display her deep interest in Mathematics and Science. Right through this period, the presence and support of the enlightened extended family gave an orientation to her personality that helped her shape her later crowded years.

The real hidden strength in Ashoka's life was her mother. The testimony *Amar Ma—Jyotirmoyee Debi* that she contributed to the collection of Jyotirmoyee Debi's writings published from the School of Women's Studies (as part of our Women Writers Reprint series) should be recalled in this context. It is worth quoting extensively from it:

At a Girl Guides camp, 1932. All her life Ashoka enjoyed the outdoors—sports, picnics and camps

> The difference in age between me and my mother was nineteen years. I cannot remember when that difference dwindled.
>
> She would give me, without hesitation, books and periodicals meant for adults to read, there was no restriction on books. In our house periodicals starting from *Sramik* to *Sabuj Patra, Kallol, Shonibarer Chithi,* down to *Nachghar* used to come. I read. Ma said, 'I will give you more books once you grow up'.[3]
>
> When I went to Jaipur after my Matriculation examination, Ma had moved away from writing poetry to essays and stories. Like Ganesh I became the copyist. The first story I copied I sent to *Prabasi* and it immediately got accepted and published in the next number.[4]

She also recounts how she helped Jyotirmoyee Debi to overcome her practice of purdah by accompanying her to various literary conventions in Delhi and other places. Once she went with her mother to a literary meet in the presence of Rabindranath Tagore and was identified as 'Jyotidi's daughter' when Tagore inquired who she was.[5]

It obviously was a mutually empowering process, as I shall have occasion to mention later, and it left an enormous influence on Ashoka, who took up women's causes with such strength and persistence. We notice in Ashoka's strongly motivated social work, a special eye for the deprived, the marginalised and sexually exploited, something that most certainly grew out of her familial bonding with her highly talented and socially committed mother. I had written in an obituary for Jyotirmoyee Debi in the *Bangla Akademi Patrika*:

> After a long life of 96 years, when she died in 1988, she was very close to the mindset of all of us women in search of emancipation.[6]

---

[3] *Jyotirmoyee Debir Rachana Sankalan* ed. Subir Roy Chowdhury, assisted by Abhijit Sen, Kolkata, Dey's Publishing & School of Women's Studies, Nov. 1991, p. 15.
[4] *Ibid.* pp. 15-16.
[5] *Ibid.* p. 15.
[6] Jasodhara Bagchi, 'Narimuktibadi Jyotirmoyee Debi' in *Bangla Akademi Patrika,* ed. Annadasankar Ray, May 1990.

Mother and daughter, 1967: 'The difference in age between me and my mother was nineteen years. I cannot remember when that difference dwindled.'

As I look back on my own enumeration of the social thrust of Jyotirmoyee Debi's writings, I recognise not only the biological mother of Ashoka, but also her true foremother in the path of strenuous service that she took up later:

> A follower of Gandhiji in the freedom struggle, this woman writer, with an all-India perspective, has taken up pen for the weaker and backward-sliding part of our society, among whom women are the foremost...The tragedy of Partition, the mental and other losses of the Partition in Bengal and Punjab, Jyotirmoyee Debi has seen through women's eyes. She has gone on pilgrimage in search of many types of men and women of our land. Having started her life within the four walls of the inner chambers, Jyotirmoyee Debi has acquainted the Bengali readers with the lives of a vast area in northern India. Many of the protagonists in her fictional writings migrate to other parts of the country in order to escape their social humiliation. Women's efforts at becoming self-reliant form a major theme in many of her novels and long stories.[7]

Much of the efforts to create opportunities for the deprived in our society that made Ashoka Gupta such a memorable persona must have owed something to this shining foremother. I cannot help thinking that the daughter's admirable work, must, in its turn, have

[7] Op. cit. p. 19.

given an incentive to her mother's extraordinary pen. This was an important process of interinanimation that John Donne talks about in a different context.

Ashoka Gupta's life journey also shows this process of give and take in an unusual context. Living always within the ambience of a large and extended family both before and after her marriage, for her social work among women and men in need blended quite easily with being part of a large family apportioning available resources, and this found a very perceptive comment in her daughter Kasturi Gupta Menon's reminiscences of her mother:

> 'Write something about Ashoka-di,' I was told. 'Not about her public work, but what she was like as a mother.' But the two strands were so entwined that I could not separate them.[8]

This is the essence of Ashoka Gupta's unique achievement in doing social work right through the days of the freedom struggle into the early years of the new millennium.

It is with this preliminary reflection on the gendered understanding of the 'Life and Work', quite inseparable in the case of Ashoka Gupta, that I turn to the main work that has been assigned to me, that is, to write an 'Introduction' to this invaluable collection of her writings and other related material carefully culled from her preserved papers by Sarmistha Dutta Gupta. Quite a lot of this material that had been preserved with care by Ashoka was originally written in Bengali. A band of dedicated translators has rendered them into English. I find this venture eminently worthwhile because it was only with patient prodding that a workaholic like her (the telling description is that of Mahasweta Debi) could be talked into writing the two books she did. *Noakhalir Durjoger Dinguli* ('the calamitous days of Noakhali') was an account of a time which she said several times marked a watershed

[8] Printed in Jadavpur University School of Women's Studies *Newsletter* no. 22 December 2008 p. 32. Reprinted below, pp. 175-186.

in a lifetime of social service. I have mentioned in my personal tribute that the late Professor Subir Roy Choudhury, a personal friend of her son Partha Sarathi Gupta, had begun the act of prodding while he and I were constant visitors in her house in connection with the publishing of selections from the writings of Jyotirmoyee Debi. The other book-length publication was her invaluable memoir *In the Path of Service* organised with great skill by her publisher-niece Mandira Sen of Stree/Samya, with help from her daughter Kasturi and niece Nilanjana, when her oral narrative was recorded, transcribed and then rendered into English. The chapterisation had to be done with her full approval. We remain grateful to the two young researchers Sipra Bhattacharya and Ranjana Das Gupta for having achieved this Herculean task and given us a most compelling narrative of what social service meant in a country unfolding as rapidly as India during the twentieth century. It was as a nonagenarian who had crossed into the new millennium that Ashoka Gupta did this breathtaking act of reminiscence.

There is no denying that these are substantial works. But I feel very happy that the following two generations have not been satisfied only with these two publications but have decided to bring out a more varied collection of her writings, photographs and other such items from her carefully preserved papers. While working with her on her mother's writings, I had been deeply struck by Ashoka's tremendous concern to preserve old papers. It would have been a pity if some of it were not carefully placed in the public domain to enable us to savour the unflagging energy and selfless dedication that she brought to the world of social work.

The two essays on the rationing system, of both food and cloth, that was introduced by the British during the war years show how determinedly she was going to use her ability in the domestic front to articulate her trenchant critique of the unnecessary hardship that was inflicted on Indian families by our rulers, often unfamiliar with the exact nature of the requirements of typical Bengali families. With relentless mustering of exact figures, weights and measures she exposes the inappropriateness of the allotments and actual distribution of food and cloth.

Saibal Gupta, young ICS officer, Rajshahi, 1936

It is very interesting to observe that as a social issue the public distribution system, as rationing is called today, continues to plague the citizens of an independent country. So many years ago in British-ruled India, a 'housewife' showed her potential as a superb planner of rationing, in the detailed measurements she cited in exposing the deprivation of these families. She showed her strength as a housewife by demonstrating how much better the distribution might have been had it been left in charge of women like her, whose lives are devoted to looking after the food and clothing of their families. Sarmistha Dutta Gupta has written in her book, *Identities and Histories: Women's Writing and Politics in Bengal*, that Ashoka Gupta had stated the grounds for why she did not want her name to appear as the author of these articles. First, she was not used to appearing in print; second, her writing was a product of consultation with many housewives in Chittagong; and, finally, she was the wife of Saibal Gupta, the District Judge of Chittagong. From the District Judge himself, there is a teasing reminder, in one of the letters written to her in 1946 when she had gone to his ancestral home Bhola:

> Have you seen the current issue of *Probasi*? 'Janaika Bangali Grihini' has written again.

Behind the intimate joke of this couple dedicated to social transformation, we see the emergence of a life pledged to the uplift of the needy.

The forties of the last century, when Ashoka Gupta accompanied her ICS husband in his district postings, was the decade in which the poet Sukanta Bhattacharya wrote *Abak Prithibi* (The World of Surprise), beginning with the Second World War and leading to the Bengal Famine in 1943, the communal riots of 1946 in Calcutta and Noakhali, and Independence accompanied by the partition of Bengal and Punjab leading to waves of refugees that continued over the next decade and a half. These writings take us through her grim Noakhali days. It is a real treasure to read excerpts from Saibal Gupta's memoirs that include a copy of Ashoka's letter to Gandhiji asking for his guidance, of her urge to help the distressed women in Noakhali who were being subjected to sexual humiliation and attempts at abduction, and Gandhiji's prompt reply.

It is worth reflecting that 'abduction' of Hindu women by Muslim men, as PK Datta has written, was one of the major motifs of communal polarisation.[9] In the case of Ashoka Gupta, it was to help

[9] Pradip Kumar Datta, *Carving Blocs: Communal Ideology in Early Twentieth-Century Bengal* (Delhi: Oxford University Press, 1999).

such abducted women among the riot victims in Noakhali that she got involved in extending relief, both material and psychological. She extended herself for the distressed population, to give them courage not to flee from their own village and habitation.

This invaluable experience of overcoming fear and living in riot-infested areas with a daughter barely two years old turned Ashoka into a unique social worker who, with a few other individuals, was to dominate the early decades of independent India not only in Bengal but at an all-India level. The exposure to human suffering and loss, taking big risks, made her the wonderful organiser of relief and rehabilitation for which there is live testimony in her piece on Dandakaranya that is published in this book.

Ashoka was not only a social worker. She very soon rose to the rank of all-India leadership and became the Chairperson of the Central Social Welfare Board. Apart from this, she was a member of the Kasturba Memorial Trust, and one of the founders of SOS Children's Villages in India where, as I have experienced later, children were given real protection and care.

Her greatest commitment was to the AIWC, historically the first all-India organisation that women could call their own. She was involved with it in the 1930s, and later in the 1950s, when the Hindu Code Bill was being debated. As she travelled with her husband to different districts of West Bengal, her experience of the different branches of the AIWC was varied. It was in Dhaka that she had first become an activist in the AIWC, something she continued all through her life. Her reminiscences as a past President give us interesting insights into this life. Her essays on family violence and women and the one on law and caring for the aged bring out the probity and conscientiousness of her observation of women's social needs, which I find entirely relevant today.

As is eloquently brought out in her memoirs, her deep involvement in the joint family made her both caring and sharing in a significant way, that actively contributed to her own brand of social work. What I have marvelled at is that she did not let this commitment turn her into a 'traditionalist' (*prachina*) in order to counter the challenges of the new (*nabina*) woman. There was a kind of robust reaching out to

Jasodhara Bagchi, Syeda Hameed, Ashoka Gupta, Shobhana Ranade and Manorma Bawa (standing) at the AIWC Annual Conference, Kolkata, 2006

the young, which kept her open to changes. A particular combination of the old and the new made her a somewhat original pathmaker. Somehow her involvement in the physical energy of the Girl Guides movement, her love of sports, her enormous ability to take on physical strain like 'walking ten miles in three hours', made her reaching out to the marginalised and deprived special and unique. The extracts from her writings will bring alive this intrepid crusader for human well-being.

Her humane tributes to her 'sisters-in-arms' as she calls them, bring out the modesty of this tireless seeker of women and children's welfare.

This book published to mark her birth centenary will be a moving reminder of this exceptional personality, whom I had the privilege to know.

Ashoka Gupta (November 8, 1912 – July 8, 2008)

In Her Words

Ashoka Gupta, 1955

This essay was written by Ashoka Gupta in her last years, looking back on the sense of fulfilment she had felt from the age of 31, when she discovered her true vocation…

The Joys of Social Service

A skeletal child hardly breathing! If one were to rescue such a child from beside the dead bodies of its parents, and re-infuse the pulse of life into its body, would not that feel as if the impossible had been made possible? Innumerable such children, taken from the jaws of certain death during the Bengal Famine of 1943, were brought to us, and we helped the life force return to their bodies little by little. On observing their smiles, their indulging in games with their thin, wasted limbs, their famished selves wolfing down meals, we broke into smiles ourselves. Whether those smiles were of gladness, success or fulfilment is rather difficult to explain! At that time it had seemed to me that there could not be any work or responsibility more important that this. Today—so many years later—when some of the children of Bankura's Shishusadan, now strong and healthy young people, meet me and call out *Ranga-Ma,* and stand in front of me, I cannot recall what they used to look like in those times. But the same joy fills my heart even now. I think to myself, if I hadn't looked after them, someone else would have. When they were fated to live, they would definitely have been saved. But I would have been denied this feeling of joy!

Thinking of these children brings back other memories too. After Partition, hordes of refugee families arrived from East Pakistan and began to live in *bustees* in Calcutta's Beleghata. At that time there were no employment possibilities or initiatives available to them. In the Miyabagan *bustee* of Beleghata, we used to keep the adults engaged with making papad, spinning wool and adult education and

Every child's Didima

the children with studies and various games. Nationally renowned women leaders used to come and visit us from time to time to take stock of the rehabilitation and relief work. This centre was run by the All India Women's Conference (AIWC). Those who came to visit would often leave some money with us to buy sweets for the children. And we would arrange *luchi-mishti* for everyone, young and old.

Many years after this, I visited the Payalkot area of Dandakaranya in 1967. That year the crops had turned out well along the new embankment. We met two young boys, very interested in trying out new farming methods. When the time came for us to return to Calcutta, they said that their father—an old man now—wanted to meet us. They kept asking us to visit their house. They also said that their father had heard a lot about us from their mother. I was taken aback. I said, 'I live in Calcutta and you live here. How does your mother know anything about me?' Be that as it may, the two boys would not take no for an answer, and I had to visit their home.

At their house, their aged father—with great humility—informed me that if I had not protected his wife and sons from certain starvation, he would not have had the good fortune of enjoying such peace and happiness in his last days. This was why he was so eager to meet me.

Just then, a woman entered carrying refreshments and touched my feet. A married woman, her head covered with the end of her sari. She looked up at me, smiled and asked, 'Don't you recognise me? You had given me work in your school in Miyabagan *bustee* in Calcutta. I used to make papad, and these sons of mine—Jhontu and Montu—used to study in the school. I am Kamala.' It was as if the distance of seventeen years was lifted instantaneously. I recognised Kamala. She was with us for about two years, and I hadn't been able to find out where she went after that. People used to say she had gone back to her village. The two youths seemed to suddenly become the young Jhontu and Montu. The younger one laughed and said, 'Don't you remember, Mashima? Pandit Mashima had come and we all ate *luchi, bonde* and *alur dum*?' Gradually the memories came flooding back. Of course—Vijaylakshmi Pandit had visited us! And Urmila Mehta too. And we had organised a meal for them one day. The first taste of *luchi-mishti* was still fresh in the young man's mind!

We had long forgotten the details, but the fact that Kamala and her sons had found safe shelter in Calcutta during those two-three years of tribulation immediately after Partition was a great boon as far as Kamala's family was concerned. Her husband told me that at that time it wasn't possible to keep his family in their native village in East Pakistan. So he had sent them to Calcutta, and after two or three years when things improved he had brought them back home. But later they had had to leave their village once again. Their wandering finally came to an end in 1964 when they settled in Dandakaranya. It was a wonderful experience—sitting there on the raised ground in front of their tin-roofed house and listening to them. Just a helping hand at the right moment had been enough to make the whole family stand on their own feet. They did not talk about their trials in those difficult years, but instead remembered eating *luchi-mishti*! Not an earth-shattering event at all, but it feels good to think about it.

In the field of social service, just as one cannot ignore the social problems in general, ignoring individual/personal problems does not really lead to much progress. Overlooking the needs of a few people or even one person in the name of the greater common good burdens the mind. And until a way out is found for a particular problem, this sense of dissatisfaction remains. Once when we were training our village workers, one of the girls fell ill and had to be hospitalised. A couple of months later, she recovered fully and was released, but the training centre did not take her back. And for all practical purposes, she had no family. So there was no place for her at home either. Her first letter to me read: 'I am completely well, but there is neither place nor work for me in my family. Do I not have the right to wish to live like a human being? If I was incapable, would I have been selected for the training in the first place? Please do reply to my questions.'

I had no reply to offer, since she was perfectly right. Two weeks later, after trying very hard, I managed to have the girl come back to us. Finally she was absorbed into the 'Nirasroy Abasan' ('home for the homeless') run by us. Every year I used to get a letter or two from her. In her last letter, she wrote, 'I can finally see the light of hope. If you, *Mashima*, had not stood by me at that time, I would not have been able to fight back and establish myself today.' The girl, though in very difficult circumstances, had managed to get a BA degree and had even secured a good job. All through her own determination and hard work. This letter fills me with happiness and fulfilment.

While going through some old papers, I came across a postcard with a note in an unsteady and elongated hand. An old man, Subhendra Kumar Bose, had written, 'I was very worried about my wife and daughter. I did not have the capacity to do anything for them. But you made arrangements for them, so now I am at peace. I express my thanks to you in this letter, in case I am not able to meet you personally before my death.' Within a month of this, the gentleman passed away. Even though I have disposed of several such letters, this one somehow survived among my papers. And, in fact, I still remember the old gentleman's appearance clearly.

Many people can and do extend a helping hand to others but if we expect something from them in return—never mind gratitude—it becomes problematic. Therefore, true happiness for a social worker comes only when work is done purely for the sake of service and not with the expectation of any return. It is a bonus if one gets appreciated and is thanked in the process. Every year, elections are held for the various posts of social welfare organisations, and new presidents, secretaries and treasurers take on responsibilities. Since each worker has to work within a timeframe in a certain field, every year their work is evaluated and the organising committee gives them a combined vote of thanks annually. This is routine in any organisation. Those who have worked hard and well, as well as those who have not, receives this vote of thanks equally. So a social worker does not really get any extra satisfaction out of this since it is just a formality. Those who really want to work towards redressing a social problem with dedication and empathy, have to plan well and spend their entire lives working on it. And just as a programme is taking shape and progressing meaningfully, it is not surprising to find a committed worker being sidelined by those who are supposed to be colleagues! The empathetic social worker does not have time to form cliques; for her the work itself is immensely rewarding! So it often happens that in the desire for power and organisational positions, several opportunists who do not actually have either competence or dedication, usurp projects run by truly empathetic workers. In such circumstances, social work does not breed joy; there is only helplessness and despair.

As I recall all this, I think to myself that my life is now drawing to a close, and my capacity for work has also reduced. After being a social worker for so many years, have I actually achieved anything worthwhile? And have I received something that will remain forever a source of constant joy? I have no doubt about the answer to this question. The most rewarding and memorable period of my working life was spent in Noakhali in 1946 when I worked for eight continuous months among the riot victims there. This was memorable for me not because we were providing relief, or setting up hospitals and schools or helping in the planning and construction of roads. The work was fulfilling because we were trying to bring human beings closer to each other. We were trying to build bridges between people, between communities. We were trying on the one hand to bring about an attitudinal change among the strong, and on the other helping the weak become strong and courageous.

All this would never have been possible and I would have been deprived of this incredible experience that filled me with a sense of fulfilment and purpose, had I not had the opportunity of coming into contact with Gandhiji and working under his direction and with his blessing. I learnt some very important lessons here and this has been the most rewarding experience in my life in social service.

Unpublished and undated article found in Ashoka Gupta's private papers

Translated by Vikram Iyengar

In Krishnanagar, 1942. After her marriage, even as she took on the responsibilities of running a joint family establishment, she saw the role of a social worker for herself. She worked tirelessly during the terrible Bengal Famine of 1943. Since 1936, she had been a member of the AIWC of which, fifty years later, she was to become the all-India President

After the terrible distress in the year of the Bengal Famine, and with the Second World War not yet over, the government introduced rationing. Ashoka Gupta, sensitive to the hardships faced by lower middle-class families as well as being concerned with her own household expenses, wrote three articles for Probasi *on the subject.*

Cloth Rationing and the Bengali Household

A Certain Bengali Housewife[10]

The food crisis has kept us so distracted for the past few days that we were almost about to forget the cloth crisis. Especially, with the coupons already collected, now clothes could be bought when convenient, one by one, for our family and relations—such was the idea. However, a government notice, issued a few days ago, has left us alarmed and worried. Twenty yards of cloth have been allotted to each person in Bengal. Further, for children below twelve years only half of this amount has been allotted. And even from these meagre allocations, the coupons for the first quarter will be deemed cancelled if the clothes are not bought by June. If one hears of this scheme suddenly, one may well wonder, what's the problem with it? If a family could do without these clothes for six months, why ever will they be needed in the seventh month? So what is lost if five yards of cloth from one quarter are cancelled?

Those who do not have in-depth knowledge of the ways in which lower-middle-class and middle-class families in Bengal earn their living will never fathom the nature of the loss or how utterly miserable

---

[10] Literally, 'A Bengali Housewife.' Contributors would often conceal their identities behind the veil of such a generic name. In the course of a series of conversations with Sarmistha Dutta Gupta in May 2002, Ashoka Gupta explained why she had preferred to conceal her identity for the three articles she wrote for *Probasi*. In those days (1940s) she didn't have any skill in public speaking or writing, nor did she have enough self-confidence. Besides, she had written the articles after speaking with many ordinary housewives in Chittagong where her husband was posted as District Judge from May 1945; hence she preferred to remain anonymous. See Sarmistha Dutta Gupta, *Identities and Histories. Women's Writing and Politics in Bengal* (Kolkata: Stree, 2010), p. 52.

its consequences can be for a poor family. Enough cannot be said of the kind of distress in which young and old, one and all of this class of people have been living due to the indirect influence of the War, the inflation, and, above all, the time the food and cloth rationing system came into operation. It doesn't seem fair at all to impose a new burden on them on top of this.

Let us calculate from around the beginning of the Roman calendar and see how a poor Bengali makes ends meet with each month's income. In the course of this discussion it will also become clear at what time of the year it is possible for a Bengali householder to buy clothes for his family with hard cash.

For even those who, as government employees, get government food-rations at a low price, four relatives would not be considered part of a single family—whatever be the actual number of members in the family. But in Bengali households, it is virtually impossible to abide by such hair-splitting calculations over the number of relatives staying. I sincerely hope that while following the government's instructions, Bengalis will never end up behaving irresponsibly towards their parents and brothers and sisters. Anyway, I assume each potential earner provides for at least six to seven dependents, keeping my estimate on the lower side.

In January, children pass their examinations and are promoted to a higher standard, a few have to be admitted to school, to say nothing if there's a boy in the family sitting an university examination. His father, or guardian, then goes virtually bankrupt buying his books, paying the fees, and arranging for new stationery. Then they have to wait for the month after, when they would again get some cash in their hands. Not only service-holders, but also lawyers, attorneys, doctors, shopkeepers—everyone is in the same boat in January. The question of buying new clothes in this month cannot arise at all for anyone. In February, too, the effect of buying new books and stationery lingers on for some time. The fees for the examinee's coaching class[11] or private tutor (who cannot be kept the whole year, but

[11] Some of the English words and phrases that appear in the Bengali text have been underscored here by the translator.

must be appointed for at least three months to help the candidate pass) have to be paid; some expenses are also incurred while making donations, either in the form of money or something else, for the Saraswati Puja. In this month, school-going boys and girls must have new clothes, so about five yards from the ten yards allotted to them may be bought with much difficulty. After much calculation, out of this cloth a frock, or a shirt and even a pair of pyjamas may be made.

It is out of the question to incur any extra expenses in March. It is the month of Chaitra in the Bengali calendar,[12] and the account books are updated at the year's end. And after all, it is only because people let us have things on credit that most of us can just about maintain the semblance of a decent life. But the creditors must be paid something, even a token amount, before they open their new account books. The grocer, the milkman, we'll be spared by no one. So in this month, too, it is impossible to buy new clothes for anyone.

In April, after paying the college fees for two whole months of a college-going brother or son, not much is left in one's hands. It is much the same in May, when two months' school fees of the children have to be paid at once. On top of that, if there's a wedding of some close relation's son or daughter in Baisakh or Jaistha,[13] then there's no other way but to seek more credit. The condition of our middle-class society is such that we are concerned more about saving our dignity than our lives. We spare no effort to make sure that no one can guess the real state of our existence. And in this fashion, the year rolls along, and May goes by.

In June, for the first time, an ordinary, educated Bengali family, living on a fixed income, is able to afford one or two sets of clothes. Maybe it is not possible to spare more than ten-fifteen rupees in this month, but then, if all the coupons of the first quarter are not used up by this month, they will be deemed cancelled. If there are six people in a family, three adults and three children, even then it will not be

[12] Chaitra is the last month on the Bengali calendar.

[13] Baisakh (beginning on April 14) and Jaistha are the first two months in the Bengali calendar.

possible for anyone to buy three outfits and seven-and-a-half metres of printed cloth all together. So far as our experience goes, we have seen that middle and lower-middle class working Bengali families buy, a little at a time, whatever cloth they need in June, July, August and September. The number of buyers soars during the Puja, and after the Puja till the month of June, Bengali families do not have much to do with cloth shops.

That if food rations are not collected one week, they cannot be picked up the following week, is something one understands: after all, it is not possible to eat double the amount in one single week! But after patiently wearing darned and mended clothes for six months, just when one is able to afford new clothes, that they cannot be bought—what sort of a situation is this? Since the total allotment is twenty yards (in the suburbs it is relatively less), the consumers should be able to buy this amount anytime they wish in the course of the year: what objection can the cloth-rationing department possibly have to this arrangement? And the cloth will be brought with hard cash, and not in excess of the amount that has been stipulated. So we fail to understand why the public should be deprived of such a facility.

Apart from Calcutta, in those suburban towns where cloth rationing has started, neither have the cloth-folders been distributed nor have the people got the coupons. The public does not know how many yards of cloth they will be getting each year, and the authorities can't tell them anything clearly. On paper it says twenty yards, but the authorities say it will probably be twelve yards, while those who are over-enthusiastic and have secured the coupons after applying for them on their own initiative, say, 'We've got at least one coupon each (for five yards or one set of clothes), but we don't know whether we'll get any more.'

I know of two-three suburban towns where such a situation has prevailed from last March (1945) till this March. No one knows how many yards of cloth people in these places will get, where they will get it from, or who they will have to appeal to in order to secure a set of cloth-coupons easily. I know of so many rural women who used to come to the city to earn a living by making *khoi* and *muri*[14] or by threshing paddy. Today, their source of income is about to be stalled simply because they do not have clothes to decently cover themselves with. I have been disturbed by their abject pleas asking me to help them get hold of tickets for clothes. When I asked them if they have ration cards, I was told that the rationing-system has not yet started in their village, and so they do not have cards, and since they do not have cards, they are not eligible to file applications to collect the coupons. I have heard that under the supervision of the Union Board there is a scheme for selling many commodities and clothes included in the ration list in the villages. There is also a Food Committee to help with these matters, but then, what is the extent of their power? My feeling is that the Food Committee can give advice, but whether it will be heeded or not is entirely left to the whims of the ration department. If anyone criticises the ration department's plans, its officials become furious. On paper, the accounts remain immaculate, even work goes on in full flow in the offices. But there is a flaw at the root of the supply department, real needs are not fulfilled by it, it is unable to supply even essential commodities to the common people.

Those who have secured that rare thing called coupons in the suburban areas are not to be envied either. I know of a family who got ten coupons for its ten members in the third week of March. So the ration cards were duly signed and the coupon numbers were noted on them. The women of the house were very excited, a few saris, dhotis, printed fabrics for dresses and so on, could be bought at last. First, the servant went from shop to shop and came back. All the shops are out of stock, the supplies will come the following week. Four-five days later, when the man was sent again, the shopkeepers reported that excellent material for shirts, *panjabis*[15] etc had arrived, the bales would all be opened the following day, and even voile has been delivered. The following day, the lady of the house went, wishing to inspect, select and buy the cloth herself. The supplies were opened. But the bale which was supposed to have the material for

[14] *Khoi* and *muri* are prepared from rice and often eaten as staple in rural Bengal.
[15] A loose shirt (*kurta*) worn by men.

shirts was stuffed with cloth meant for umbrellas, and in the one that was supposed to have voile, there was velvet (*shalu*). The dhotis were all nine cubits,[16] forty-two inches long, and although the saris were twelve cubits in length, they were only forty-two inches in width. And then again they were of a rather flimsy quality. But even so, these were not cheap. Each sari cost almost five rupees (earlier, one could get a Dhanekhali or a Santipuri sari at this price), while the dhotis were two rupees and twelve annas each. As a result, nothing could be bought; the coupons were valid only up to 31st March, and so they were all wasted. This is not just one isolated incident; I have seen such incidents repeating themselves many times over in front of my eyes. The cloth-rationing department does not know what is being supplied to the shopkeepers, the shopkeepers do not know what is there in the bales, and before the consumer has even begun to understand the real story, the coupons have been cancelled.

Then the district rationing authorities put all the blame on the Calcutta office. Apparently, the latter does not supply things according to demand. The subdivisional authorities say that bale after bale full of things that are not popular in the villages arrive at the subdivisions. On seeing the quality of the thin voile, fine dhoti and good quality cloth for coats, and hearing their price, villagers avert their faces and walk away. For a few days, these things remain hoarded in the subdivisions, and only the supply department knows if they are sent back to the warehouses afterwards. The employees on duty at the cloth-rationing department have very vague ideas about what kind of cloth is needed for what purpose, what their names are and how much their demand is. 'Shirting', 'coating', 'longcloth', and dhoti-sari are all that they understand, more or less. But they are not aware of the fact that shirting could refer to virtually anything, from cloth meant for umbrellas to coarse, double-threaded cloth (*doshuti*), to even thick textiles of all kinds meant for sofas, cushions, curtains, coach cushions and drill saddle. They are not mistaken about longcloth, but many of them don't know what the '*markin*' (American) kind is. By *kora*, or unbleached cloth, they

[16] One cubit is roughly equivalent to the indigenous unit, one *haath*.

only understand 'grey'. When there is demand for white drill, the ration department says—'It's not there'. But white drill, unbleached, is being sold as 'grey drill' in the shops.

Those white men who, as heads of district ration departments, are engaged in solving the cloth crisis have even more fascinating notions of what Bengalis wear. Once last year, a 'permit' was requested to buy standard cloth for poor girls in an ashram run by women. The female superintendent had applied for twelve pieces of cloth, eight of them saris and four dhotis. The dhotis were meant for the widows. The sahib, who was at the helm of the ration department of that district, refused the permit. He wrote that while it was understandable that saris had been asked for a girls' ashram, it was incomprehensible why dhotis should be given as well. Needless to say, the white employee did not grant the permit. The lady in charge of the ashram wrote him a detailed letter, in which she tried her best to explain the custom of wearing dhotis or *thaans*[17] among Hindu widows in Bengal, and reapplied for the permit. But all her efforts were in vain. The sahib, it seemed, was stubbornly resolved not to understand anything. Finally, not only were the dhotis not obtained but the permit for the saris also never arrived. The widows had, for that matter, agreed to wear saris, but thanks to the decree of the white boss of the cloth-rationing department, they were not able to get even that. To end the cloth crisis faced by the girls, the ashram had to appeal to a Marwari, who was distributing standard cloth after getting a cloth permit.

White *thaan* is still rarely available, thin-bordered ten-cubit dhotis are not very usual either, and nine-and-a-half cubit dhotis do not suffice for women. We have no qualms in making the claim that the cloth-rationing system has created a greater inconvenience for Bengali women. It is possible to make do with twenty yards of cloth or four saris every year with some difficulty, but what about chemises and girls' dresses? At two-and-a-half yards per chemise, at least ten more yards of cloth are needed by urban women. Ten yards have been allotted to children below twelve. If these ten

[17] *Thaan* is a length of white cloth traditionally worn by Hindu widows.

yards are measured out, cut and stitched at home, meticulously and judiciously, then three half-pants and three half-shirts[18] may barely be made out of them. But most boys cannot make do with three pants a year and saris for growing girls cannot be made at all out of ten yards of cloth. As for the younger girls, it is doubtful whether three frocks, three pyjamas and one chemise can be made out of ten yards (if the width is not sufficient). It is not possible for the men of the family to make do with twenty yards of cloth; for, apart from dhotis, shirts and *panjabi*s are also needed by them. Besides, there are bed sheets, pillow covers and hundreds of other essential commodities on which the authorities seemed not to have spared a thought while setting up the rationing system.

There is one particular matter that we women often discuss among ourselves. Everyone knows that once a baby is born there is no provision for separate clothes for it. Yet many are aware that due to the present clothes deficiency, bed linen and clothes for a newborn pose a great problem. Earlier, old clothes could be used to make *kanthas*[19] and so on, but now, when the mother herself does not get enough to wear, where will the old clothes for the child come from? A newborn's need for clothes is not small: even in the absence of *kanthas*, there must be some eight or ten sheets, a few tunics, pillows, bed linen—which of these can be done away with? Is it too much to allot twenty yards of cloth for a newborn and its mother? In England, there is a provision for issuing special coupons to expecting mothers. Thus the mother is able to secure clothes that will be needed by her baby even before it is born. If in our country a suitable amount of *markin* cloth or longcloth can be bought for children, then mothers will be spared many troubles.

As it is, don't mothers have plenty of problems already? They have domestic errands to run, they have to think up ways of providing the family with four square meals out of meagre rations and a limited income, and even if they are able to finish all the daily chores, there is no respite for their hands, which are kept busy with needle and thread.

---

[18] Referring to shorts and half-sleeved shirts respectively.

[19] *Kanthas* used to cover babies are usually made from pieces of soft, old cloth.

Under the system run by the ration department food and clothes have become rarities these days. Since they are difficult to get hold of, most of us have to waste a lot of time in collecting them. Further, since the supply is always less than the demand, many are not averse to buying them on spec or at a higher price in the black market. Do we not realise that with each day our sense of right and wrong is diminishing? We are full of contempt for black marketeers but if an unscrupulous businessman tries to sell us, on credit, ten *seers* of sugar or ten yards of cloth keeping a slight profit for himself, will we not be tempted?

Yet it is not difficult to erase the desire to buy things from black marketeers from the hearts of the common people. If people are not given food and clothes according to their needs, they will of course flock to the black marketeers' doors to obtain what they lack. But if suitable amounts of food and cloth are allotted to them, their needs will be answered and the racketeering will also diminish.

But I wonder for how long we will be suffering from this want of food and cloth. Unless this situation is remedied urgently, all will be lost for Bengalis.

First published as 'Bastro Rationing O Bangali Songsar'
('Rationing of Clothes and the Bengali Family')
in *Probasi*, Baisakh 1352 BS (April-May 1945)

Translated by Somak Ghoshal

Ashoka Gupta, 1962

Ashoka Gupta's concern for the condition of housewives under the rationing system and other wartime measures is evident in this article that she wrote for Probasi.

Rationing and the Bengali Housewife

A Certain Bengali Housewife[20]

It is evident from the daily and monthly British papers that people in that country are urgently discussing the inconveniences that are being faced by housewives under the present rationing system and other wartime measures. Some are pointing out the deficiencies of the rationing system in letters to the editor; some are writing articles suggesting ways in which husbands, children and other family members can be fed on the meagre rations; while some, based on their own understanding of the situation, are indicating ways in which the flaws in the rationing system can be eradicated. I don't know what the outcome of all this writing is. Do the officials of the supply department really look into the difficulties of the housewives and try to mend the problems? Or is all this writing entirely in vain?

If one were to judge by the example of what goes on in this country, one would have to admit that writing in newspapers is indeed quite meaningless. Since the rationing system came into being to date, such a lot of debate, discussion, complaints and opposition on the merits and demerits of the system have appeared in daily, monthly, Bengali, English, in papers of all kinds. But who could wash off the stain that has once tainted the government offices? On the basis of this observation, it seems that Bengali housewives have desisted from

[20] See footnote no. 10 on page 33.

writing even a few lines in the papers about their bitter experience of struggling to make ends meet because they know full well that it is quite fruitless to cry in the wilderness. And even if anything were to be gained, when do these women have the time to put their grievances and complaints in writing, when their days are spent worrying over the current rationing system and working hard to extract provisions from it so as to be able to give their husbands and children enough to eat?

In the big cities, where rationing has begun, rice, flour, sugar, salt and, since the last few months, mustard oil are available. Till now, not much could be said against the quantity of rice and flour made available, though in the city of Calcutta and elsewhere, all classes of people were astonished by the quality of the rice. As for the flour, it could not be touched, and is still thus. I have asked women of all strata, living in the village and the city, and all of them have told me that they have never in their lives cooked rice of such appalling quality.

But even if sack after sack of rotten rice emerges and the public are forced to eat this rice from the storehouse of the supply department, there is no one to punish the storekeepers. On top of that, the food experts of the civil supplies department may even issue a certificate stating that people are indeed used to eating rice of such quality. We women in amazement think that, after all, we have spent most of our lives in the kitchen and the pantry, cleaning up, sorting and storing the year's provision of rice, lentils and spices, apart from coping with a hundred other domestic chores. We have put these provisions out in the sun, and got them back in again at the right time, careful not to let things get too old, not letting even a handful of semolina go to waste. Yet, this large granary is meant to store merely rice, wheat, some small portions of lentils, sugar and salt, for which it has as large a number of employees, present continuously from ten to five, getting a fat salary precisely for this purpose, and still there is no end to the wastage. Many have noticed that often government advertisements are published on how to fill up vacant posts, how to prevent rats from eating up the provisions, how to keep them dry and fresh, and so on. Who are these advertisements meant for? If they are meant for us, then our answer will be this: we have been learning, since our earliest years, how to preserve things and nothing ever goes to waste in our households. And how will things get wasted anyway? A week's ration is bought, and is over in seven days; what's left that can be hoarded? And if these advertisements are meant for the farmers, they would do well to remember that the farmers have known how to protect the fruits of their labour since time immemorial, and farmers in our country are anyway in no situation to let things go to waste. If these measures are meant for the entrepreneurs, then the answer is that out of their own selfish interest they take all sorts of precautions so as not to suffer losses on what they have in the warehouses. Perhaps the advertisements are intended for the government agents who buy the provisions, and for the supervisors of the department's warehouses? If that is the case, then the easiest thing would be to have a few official circulars printed and sent to the right places. Why waste the taxpayers' money on advertisements? And in any case, even after all these advertisements, we have not been spared the rotten flour and old, foul-smelling rice.

But we had become used to just about anything almost. Although fuel and time galore would be wasted trying to cook rice that is three years old, and the food would turn out to be tasteless, it would at least fill stomachs. Now we fail to fathom how we will make do with the two *seers* and twenty ounces[21] that have been allocated per head. We are unable to get milk, we cannot afford to buy fish, we haven't seen fruits in ages, we depend on rice, lentils and vegetables (and very little of the latter) to appease the hunger of our own families and relatives—what shall we do now? Since we have to do all the arduous tasks at home, we must eat a full lunch of rice in the afternoon. Widows are supposed to eat once a day, so they must have a full meal just that once. Additionally, in most Bengali families young boys usually eat rice after coming home from school. As a result, in the afternoon one has to cook, on an average, ten ounces of rice per head. In the evening, one needs to prepare another six ounces on an average. If anything less than this amount is cooked, some will be forced to

[21] Two ounces = a chattack. The Indian units of measure are: 16 chattacks = 1 *seer*; 40 *seers* = 1 maund.

remain half-fed. The man of the family cannot be given less to eat; the children too must be given a full meal; so does that mean that under the new rationing system it is we women who must remain half-fed and forgo our share?

Except for the ration department, everyone else seemed to be aware of the fact that boys and girls eat like full-grown adults from the time they are around eight or nine years old; sometimes they eat even more. With their growing bodies, they do need to eat a substantial amount. But so far under the rationing system they used to get only half that amount. We don't know for what good deed of ours it has been decided that boys and girls would be entitled to full rations from the age of eight. It could be worse. But needless to say, a meagre two *seers* and twenty ounces cannot satisfy the needs of children who have to study and do physical labour, and are not in a position to afford fish, milk or eggs. Even if one were to avoid scientific calculations based on calories, common sense and first-hand experience should be enough to tell us that with this quantity of food intake the next generation of Bengali children will be short-lived and suffer from malnutrition; when in years they will mature, they will have little physical strength; and in the future they will bear witness to the dire consequences of the rationing system of 1946. Given the meagre quantities of rice and wheat available, Bengali girls will from time to time have to starve. Then, the ration shops remain closed on all the government holidays. Let us assume that Monday is the day on which the rations have to be fetched. Suddenly, on Saturday, a notice appears in the papers that the shops will remain closed on Monday, Tuesday and Wednesday for some special occasion. Since it is impossible to survive for more than seven days on the quantity of rations allocated, what other way remains than to fast for three consecutive days?

It would be universally admitted that flour is not a particular favourite with Bengalis. As it is, Bengali boys and girls don't want to eat too many *rotis*; they like and crave for rice. Still, if only the quality of the flour were better, or it were regularly available, then it would have suited everyone to eat *roti* during the day, since rice is so scarce. But wheat and flour are stored with such utter lack of care that they get spoiled even before they reach the market. As a result, everyone, especially we women ask whoever's going to pick up the rations not to get flour. Why should we spend good money on rotten food and give it to our children, especially when it takes so much longer to make *rotis*? Even so, we could have cut down on rice, would have eaten as many *rotis* as possible, had we been assured that the surplus food would reach those who really need it.

During the famine of 1943, many housewives in Calcutta and in the suburbs had the experience of having to give away food to the hungry. I know for a fact that even in very poor families women had eaten a little less in order to feed one or two hungry mouths, and seldom had anyone turned away those who came to them expecting food. There is a sense of self-satisfaction in this act of charity, and the one who gives feels an awakening of a sense of duty and responsibility within. In every household, there is a daily practice of setting aside a handful of rice to be given away in charity, before starting the day's cooking. For so long, in spite of our own dire needs, we have been able to give to others, and have realised how essential it is to do so. During the last famine, women in each neighbourhood had come together to organise communal cooking to feed the starving. Now, under the new rationing scale, the impulse to worry about others beyond worrying about oneself will be on the verge of extinction. We will have to turn away the hungry disappointed, perhaps even deprive them of a handful of rice, we will refuse to take note of our starving neighbours, and shoo away beggars with harsh words. For the lack of an alternative, we will be forced to act in ways that go against our good conscience, if only for the sake of our husbands and children.

Apparently, with the new per-head quota which has come into force since the middle of March, there will be a surplus of 165,000 maunds[22] of foodgrain in greater Calcutta, according to government estimates. And ostensibly, based on this arrangement it will be possible to give away two-and-a-half *seers* of food to 264,000 people every week. But who is going to disburse it? During the last famine, we have seen people dying of hunger in village after village, but even though stocks of rice existed on paper and in calculations, the rice had not reached

[22] See footnote no. 21 on page 45.

the people. Though locked away in the warehouses, the sacks could not unbind themselves from the red tape and reach the public in time. In station after station, in the Botanical Garden, in the warehouses of the suburban agents, rice was lying around. But for this rice to reach the common man there were so many impediments along the way that save for those officials with infinite patience, nobody could make any headway in that direction, and ultimately, most of the officials failed in their mission. Those who have some experience of relief work will know how many applications and requests have to be made to any organisation in order to secure rice for relief purposes, and even when permission is secured, what a great deal of expense, time and patience are involved in depositing the money in the treasury, getting hold of the receipt (*challan*), and then arranging for the rice which is stowed away in some remote warehouse to be delivered to the city. Often, it is never available in time. In many cases, one gets rice of far inferior quality and price than was promised. Then it is too late to seek a refund from the treasury, and there's no way of exchanging the rice for one of better quality. For these various reasons, we have grave doubts about what is shown on paper as surplus rice ever reaching the public in times of need. One imagines it would not only be that villagers would die of starvation, but that those of us who are grateful for being eligible to draw rations—that is to say, the city-dwellers—would also remain half-fed and half-dead. In the meantime, the rice languishing in the government godowns will become infested with pests and the official logbooks will go on recording tonnes of surplus rice.

To come to sugar and salt, it makes no sense to allot a *poa*[23] of salt per head, no one can eat a *seer* of salt in a month, so it would have done no harm to allot a little less of it. Till the time one could get one-and-a-half *poa* of sugar per head in Calcutta, probably nobody had to go seek out the black market. But any housewife will know how difficult it is to make do with just a *poa* of sugar. If there are infants drinking only milk at home, one would need more than a *poa* of sugar per child, and that is how it should be. But then, what do our children ever get to eat or enjoy? Who spares a thought for them

[23] One *poa* = a fourth of a *seer*.

anyway? This, after all, is not Britain, where even during the war, in every school arrangements were made for all children below five to have orange juice and cod-liver oil. Here, even a bit of sugar with milk is impossible to secure. Yet many may not be aware how much sugar is being sent to Britain every week in gift parcels. If you keep an eye on the 'Letters' section of *The Statesman*, you will find people who had sent tea, sugar, butter, soap, paneer etc in gift parcels to Britain writing in, at least once a week, to lament the fact that these gifts had all got spoiled en route. Any British gift-parcel sender can send one or more of the above items in a parcel weighing up to three-and-a-half *seers*. No harm in sending one every day, for that matter, as long as they are addressed to different names. As one such person was about to send off a parcel, he was told, 'Don't you know India is facing a food crisis and famine?' He retorted, 'Don't you know, there isn't any ghee available to fry our cutlets or sugar for our cakes? That women at home are living in great misery?' He sent off a few pounds of coco, jam and sugar. Just calculate it once and work it out: if even hundred foreigners send one parcel each to Britain every week, then three hundred and fifty *seers* of food go out of the country. Has anyone any idea how many such parcels are being sent out of the country by how many thousand British people? At least those of us who are living in the ration-eligible areas get one *poa* sugar every week, but sugar doesn't even reach the villages, and in the district towns, maybe three *seers* of sugar are allotted to families with twelve members.

And what can one possibly say of mustard oil! Whoever had given half a *seer* of mustard oil per person every month must be immeasurably ignorant, especially if he happens to be Bengali. Ask any Bengali housewife—from a family of a daily-wage-earner or farmer, from a middle-class, lower-middle class or wealthy family—and she will tell you how this paltry allocation has caused her untold misery. Even someone who never indulges in any luxury likes to use a little oil on the body and head. We cannot think of bathing a baby without applying oil. We have seen that those children who don't get enough to eat feel much better in body and mind if they get a little oil to put on their bodies. But given the allotment of oil, we had to stop applying oil on the body and head; cooking, too, has been reduced to preparing boiled or grilled food (a bit of oil is needed here too). Before fixing the allotment of oil had the authorities taken the trouble to go into the inner chambers once and ask their respective wives, they would have found out how much oil should be required every month. Does nobody know what constitutes food for the poor Bengali? We are unable to buy ghee, cannot afford to get milk, can seldom get hold of eggs or fish. It is only mustard oil that acts as fat or fatty substance in the list of the food items that we can choose from. Is it so difficult to calculate that if 16 ounces are allotted per head how little a person would get to consume of fat and fatty substances every day? If our children do not get even a little spoonful of oil every day, how are they going to keep well? And how many are in a position to buy bottles of olive oil and coconut oil at two, two-and-a-half rupees to anoint their bodies?

If this allotment-system stays on even for a few months, then I can say on behalf of Bengali women that very soon boys and girls and babies would without question be afflicted with various diseases.

I have asked daily-wage earners, washermen, hawkers, gardeners, sweepers, cobblers, drivers, junior officers of the government, ordinary clerks and women of all classes in the rationed areas about the current arrangements, and I have been informed unanimously that even a ration of half a *seer* of cereals (rice or wheat) is not enough for them. If one were to have two full meals, at noon and around nine or ten at night, then half a *seer* of cereals should be sufficient. Although for the sake of the greater common good we should reduce the intake of food, on an average every person still needs three-quarter of a *seer*. We fail to understand how on earth someone who has to undertake rigorous physical labour can make do with anything less than four or four-and-a-half *seers*. I have hired day-labourers in exchange for daily meals, and I have found them polishing off half a *seer* of rice after each spell of hard work. If at least three *poas* of oil per head could be arranged, then we could have somehow thought of a way to get on with our cooking, though we would not still think of using oil on our body or head if the amount allotted per head is less than one *seer*.

Even today, I found tangled-up, pest-infested rice selling for four *seers* a rupee. Why do the authorities overseeing the rationing system not seek the opinion of farmers before storing rice and flour in the godowns? Could a dry granary with the capacity to store forty-fifty *maunds* of rice not be built? Could a *puro* modelled on the *puro* of twenty-thirty *maunds* capacity in Bankura district not be built to store rice? Is it impossible to create large *mites* with cement? In the entire area that is taken up to build godowns, hundreds of *golas* or *puros* or *mites* could have been installed. It may be convenient to keep rice in sacks, but then a lot of it gets wasted in the process. Only the experienced know how quickly the hundreds of sacks of rice that are stowed away at the bottom of the godowns get spoiled. Rice kept in sacks usually does not keep well for more than six months. If the authorities had asked those who had maintained large warehouses before the war, they would have found out how to store rice for a long time without it getting spoiled.

Perhaps the authorities will not pay any heed to our utterances. Perhaps this is only futile weeping in the wilderness. But I shudder to think of our children, the future of our nation. There is a scarcity of clothes, about which I am not too worried. But young boys emaciated by the want of food in every house, young girls with bodies lacking nutrition, babies with their lives waning due to the lack of milk—the very thought of such a picture of Bengal overwhelms the hearts of us mothers with pain.

First published as 'Rationing O Bangali Grihini'
('Rationing and the Bengali Housewife'),
in *Probasi*, Chaitra 1352 BS (March-April 1946)

Translated by Somak Ghoshal

Ashoka and her husband Saibal wrote to each other regularly when they were apart. Saibal's letters were all carefully kept by Ashoka, each in its envelope. This was written two months before India and Bengal were plunged in despair by news of the Calcutta Killings, and then the riots in Noakhali, a crisis that was going to bring Gandhiji to East Bengal and into their lives. Ashoka had seen Gandhiji once before, as a child of seven in Delhi, in 1919 during the Non-Cooperation movement.

Saibal to Ashoka

Chattogram
June 4, 1946

I am worried as I have not heard from any of you in a long while. I had sent you a letter yesterday. I had thought I would get a letter from you today, but there was nothing for me in today's mail either. There has never been such a long gap.

Nritya Gopal Basu arrived day before yesterday; he will leave this evening. He will probably not carry too much of a positive impression of our hospitality. So what? I have done my best. The rains have arrived here, announcing their arrival vociferously by flecking the skies with dark and heavy clouds early this morning. It rained all morning; it is ten now and the rain seems to have stopped for the moment. But we can still see heavy rain clouds in the sky.

Emon Dine Tare Bola Jay
Emon Ghana Ghor Barishay[24]

But the person I would bare my heart to is two hundred miles away and is so engrossed with the wedding that she does not have the time even to write a single letter. I am really anxious not having received any letter from you. Are you all well? Has some malady struck you? Have you all reached Bhola uneventfully? So many questions plague my mind. If I don't get a letter from you even tomorrow, I may send you a telegram. Then we might have the 'telegram' jests and quarrels we used to have before our marriage. Till yesterday, I was just feeling bad about not hearing from you, but today I have got really worried...

Have you read the newspaper reports talking of an imminent railway strike? You should hurry up and come here, otherwise, you may not be able to come at all...

Tell Partha *Mouchak*[25] has arrived. Have you seen the current issue of *Probasi*? *Janaika Bangali Grihini*[26] has written again. It also carries another piece written by someone from Chattogram using a pseudonym.

Love

---

[24] Romantic lines from a song by Rabindranath Tagore. A rough translation would be something like this: 'it is on such a day of dense, heavy rain that the heart can be laid bare to her.'

[25] *Mouchak* was a celebrated children's magazine.

[26] Literally 'A Bengali Housewife'—the pseudonym used by Ashoka Gupta in her articles in three issues of *Probasi*, two of which have been included in this volume.

Noakhali group, Kasturi in front, photograph by Ashoka Gupta, 1946

The defining experience of Ashoka's life—her involvement in Noakhali—is described through accounts by her huband, through her letters, through the pages of her unpublished diary, and through later recollections...

This is how Saibal Gupta recalled it.

Noakhali

The Great Calcutta Killings in August (1946) were followed by a series of smaller riots and scuffles in Chattogram. Even though the city was under military protection the tension was quite palpable. News of the Noakhali riots reached us during the Pujas.

The Noakhali riots began on October 10, 1946. The news reached us immediately through word of mouth; the newspapers reported the riots between October 17 and 20. The Congress president, Acharya Kripalani, and his wife, Srimati Sucheta, went to meet the Commissioner at his house in Chattogram to discuss the administrative measures to be taken in the riot-affected areas.

Activists of the Nikhil Bharat Nari Sammilani had started relief work at various stations under the leadership of Srimati Nellie Sengupta. On that day, October 20, Ashoka and a few other workers had gone to meet the Commissioner, Mr Carter, to discuss those very issues. Their demand was that endeavours to rescue abducted women be accelerated. 'That will take time,' Mr Carter said, 'It may take days, months, and even years before you can rescue them.'

The women activists felt angry and frustrated; they went back and decided they would do it themselves, however difficult it proved to be. They also gained confidence from Sucheta Kripalani's presence at the meeting. Then Gandhiji arrived on November 7. Activists, both men and women, irrespective of which party they owed allegiance to, started arriving in Chandpur and Chowmuhani from all corners of India. Ashoka and her friends went there as well. They all started working together. But realising that the work could not be done in this fashion, that a long-term strategy needed to be formulated, Ashoka's group wrote to Mahatmaji asking him how things could be planned and how the resistance of families could be countered.

Here is the letter that Ashoka wrote to Gandhiji:

Chattogram
December 6, 1946

Respected Mahatmaji,
You may remember that we, two women activists of the Nikhil Bharat Nari Sammilani (Chattogram branch), had met you in Chowmuhani and had made Lakshmipur our primary area and started work in the adjoining villages. Unfortunately, we could not carry on for more than fifteen days at a stretch because we both had baby children at home.

Villagers from three villages adjoining Lakshmipur, namely, (1) Gopinathpur, (2) Uttar Hamchandi, and (3) Khayajpur near Hasundi, have already been impressed by our ideas and promised to return to their original villages with us.

We do not expect you to reply to this letter. But we would be greatly obliged if you gave us an audience on the 16th or the 17th and shared your valuable advice on the matter with us.

Respectfully,
Yours sincerely,
Ashoka Gupta

The response came by the very next mail. A postcard sent by Gandhiji, typed in English.

> Dear Sister,
> Yours of the 6th instant. I take you at your word and say nothing in reply to your letter except that I shall be glad to see you, when you come and discuss things.
>
> Sd. MK Gandhi

On getting the postcard Ashoka and I left for Srirampur village in Noakhali with her fellow activist, Phullarani Das, Professor Ranendrakumar Das and a Muslim army officer who wished to accompany us. Srirampur was the last rail station on our journey to Chowmuhani; from there one had to travel by bus to Ramganj.

Gandhiji had rested and had just sat down with his charkha. He called us in when he heard of our arrival. Srijukta Sucheta Kripalani was also present there on that day. We met her as well. She stayed with us for a while. Ashoka had gone armed with many questions but all her personal problems and doubts seemed to pale into insignificance as she encountered Gandhiji's imposing personality. She could not utter a word.

'Should I speak in Hindi, or in English?' Gandhiji first asked. The women in our group were quite conversant in Hindi but that was not the case with us, the men in our group. The majority voted in favour of English. 'You should file for divorce,' Gandhiji chuckled heartily.

The ice was broken. We overcame our initial hesitation and started asking Gandhiji various questions. Ashoka and Phullarani proposed that they would visit the village alternately and each of them would work there for fifteen days before returning home for the next fifteen days. When Ashoka returned home, Phullarani would replace her for the next fifteen days and so it would go on. That way, they would not have to neglect the demands of their family and their children entirely. Mahatmaji listened to everything attentively. Then he said, 'You know, I am not one who believes in partial renunciation as a path to achieving our goals. Those who take that path believe they are doing something great and expect recognition and rewards and

Ashoka Gupta in Noakhali

feel disappointed when they fall short of their expectations. If you decide to take the path of sacrifice for your ideals, you cannot afford to harbour any attachment. You must find happiness in your work, you must put your heart and soul into your work.'

After a slight pause, he recounted the tale of Rajab Ali, a Muslim boy who had teamed up with a Hindu boy to stop the riots in Ahmedabad and had laid down his life in the process. 'That is what true conviction is. If you really believe in a cause, you must remain true to it and not waver even in the face of the ultimate sacrifice.

'You say you have small daughters. If you take them with you when you go to work in the villages, their lives too may be put in danger—such are the circumstances today. Moreover, you too must be prepared for sudden death. You cannot ask uprooted villagers to return to their own villages until you can prove that you are ready to risk the lives of your own children first.'

Ashoka and Phullarani had not realised before this that their plan of working in shifts was a sign of their lack of mental strength and was as futile as trying to travel with feet perched on two different boats. Thanks to Mahatmaji's words, they now became conscious of what had lain dormant in the recesses of their mind. But he did not embarrass them; he was probably only interested in finding out how prepared they really were.

Trouble was still flaring up here and there in Noakhali. Ashoka and her friend told Mahatmaji they had no qualms about going to the Noakhali villages. But we, that is Ranenbabu (Phullarani's husband) and I, were not ready for this; how could we, as fathers, let our children go, knowing full well that their lives might be put in danger?

'It is, of course, the duty of workers to risk their lives in trying to save the villagers, but what right do mothers have to put the lives of their innocent children on the line?' I asked.

'You see what your Lord and Master says!' Mahatmaji said, looking at Ashoka and Phullarani.

I prayed humbly to Gandhiji that I could resign from my job and be with them and join the ever-burgeoning movement if Gandhiji considered me fit for the task.

Gandhiji replied simply, 'You are saying the child cannot live away from the mother. If she cannot live away from her mother, then she must live with her mother. A child is part of the mother as long as she is dependent on her. I am happy you are volunteering as well, but at the moment I will only put your wife to work. I will call you when you are needed—you may join us then.'

The words he spoke so simply and yet so convincingly left no room for argument of any sort.

Seeing Ashoka about to respond, he told her, 'Don't take a hasty decision. You will only succeed if you can live without fear in the villages and remain a servant of Truth, otherwise all your efforts will come to nought. It is when miscreants realise you are fearless that they will treat you with respect. But you must always remember that they can distinguish between true fearlessness and mere bravado.'

'You will be going to villages from where the villagers have run away in fear,' Mahatmaji addressed Ashoka and Phullarani. 'Seeing you there will give them the courage to return. You may have to go to villages inhabited exclusively by Harijans, or villages where villagers have lost all hope. They have to be rescued from utter despair and terror. Many of them will say they are still in their village because they have faced no oppression, but I know that is not true. Follow my advice and work as I say and you will succeed, otherwise, you may not be able to come back alive. So take your time, think it over carefully and then come to a decision. You cannot look back once you take the decision. Your husband may visit you once in a while, but you cannot return home before your work is done.'

After giving it a lot of thought, Ashoka and Phullarani went back and told Gandhiji that their minds were made up and they were resolved to join the work with no reservations whatsoever. He then gave them a lot of advice about their future course of work and the kind of problems they would face.

Mahatmaji said as if in a soliloquy, 'The problem is very complex and very difficult. I had envisaged a terrible and dangerous situation, but the situation on the ground in Noakhali is even worse than that. I am hopeful that the situation will improve soon, but I am also prepared for any eventuality. Only time will tell what lies in store for us. Still, I am optimistic that life will return to normal, that the fear of riots will no longer haunt our minds, that the Muslim populace will have a change of heart soon.

'I had a great desire to leave this nightmarish situation behind, go somewhere else, and work a few more years. But I will not leave Noakhali until I can quench the embers of disquiet that continue to burn under the ashes, until I can usher in communal harmony.'

Mahatmaji continued, 'People say my presence in Noakhali is responsible for all the problems here. But that is not true. I had to rush here because there were problems. I am sure you know that what is happening in Noakhali today is symptomatic of what is happening all over India. But I will not lose hope, no matter how desperate the situation might be; I will continue to speak in favour of peace.'

Finally he said, 'If any of you submit to fear while living in these villages, then the villagers will understand you are weak because it is only the weak who are afraid. The truth is, fear is like a contagious disease—once you let it in, it spreads easily. When one man becomes afraid of another, fear assumes the proportions of an epidemic. That is why courage is the need of hour. What people do not understand is that courage, too, is infectious—one courageous person can instill courage in the hearts of a thousand men and women.' The military officer with us—let us say his name is Col. Ashraf—asked, 'This *Ramrajya* that you speak of—do you think this *Ramrajya* will become reality? What exactly is this *Ramrajya* like?' Gandhiji's answer was like this—'A country, a society where every single individual can live happily and in peace—that is our *Ramrajya*.'

Leaving Ashoka and our daughter there, I returned to Chattogram. But when cholera broke out there in April-May, 1947, Sucheta Kripalani wrote to me, 'Bring Ashoka home. Otherwise, your daughter will not survive. In any case, there is no way Partition can be avoided.'

I wrote to Ashoka:

Chattogram
May 10, 1947

> You have got us worried. We have not had any letter from you, and we are worried about how you are faring. It is difficult to deal with the doubts and questions that assail the mind.

Ashoka's reply arrived:

Tumchar Camp
May 15, 1947

> I left Baraliya camp Sunday night, but I only reached here Wednesday night, that is yesterday. There was a terrible storm and a downpour on Monday night. Sneha Kanjilal left by jeep, but the area was so muddy that travelling proved impossible and she returned at eleven at night. Pyarelal reached Duttapara with great difficulty. The jeep came back next morning. The roads were still very muddy. We had to wait till three before we could set out on our journey. We had reached Noakhali around nine in the morning. I met Jaman, McInerny and Mr Khan and had lunch at the SP's house. We reached Chowmuhani at three, and from there we set out for Lakshmipur. The moment we reached Lakshmipur we found ourselves in the midst of a terrible storm. Sneha stayed the night at Rambabu's house and reached here early in the morning. I finished

some work in Lakshmipur and set out for Duttapara at three in the afternoon by jeep. I met Nanidi and Nipenbabu there. When we reached Battoli, the driver said we had run out of fuel. Seeing no sign of a bus, Prabhat and I started walking. We reached Lakshmipur exactly at seven; then we all set out together and reached Tumchar at eight. Ten miles in three hours. Quite a *record*, what do you say?

We are fine. Kasturi is quite all right. These last eight days have seen widespread panic here. Everybody says, we have all but left. And the Muslims too organise meetings and ask us, 'What will you do now, eh? Where is all your tall talk now?' Two pairs of cows had gone missing yesterday. They have been found. People are a little unhappy because payments related to Test Relief [sic] have been held up. The CO will hold an enquiry into the matter today. Let us see what happens. It is the same story in the entire *thana*. Send me two copies of the registration [sic] by post. I shall forward it to Rebecca Ghosh of the Standing Committee. It may be a good idea to ask Rebecca Ghosh to preside over the May 21 meeting. I shall mention it; if need be, the convenor too will write.

Yours,
Ashoka

Ashoka's letter made me realise she was quite immersed in her work; she was drawing her sustenance from it and it had become a passion for her now. Ashoka and her colleagues were not in a position to realise that the country was inching towards a great crisis and that Gandhiji found himself overtaken by despair. I went to bring them back towards the end of May. They came back then, leaving only the medical unit in Tumchar.

Then, on June 3, we heard on the radio that India would be partitioned. The workers were plunged into despair when they saw all their hard work coming to nought.

Excerpted from Saibal Gupta's book, *Kichhu Smriti, Kichhu Katha*
(Kolkata: MC Sarkar and Sons, 1994)

Translated by Sayantan Dasgupta

And this was Ashoka's account, as she recalled it over half-a-century later

Noakhali 1946: Working under the Guidance of Mahatma Gandhi

It was towards the end of Ashwin (mid-Sept–mid-Oct) in 1946. We were in Chittagong. Gradually, through word of mouth and newspapers we heard heart-rending stories of Noakhali coming in. I was extremely anxious about the abducted and molested girls there. It was a time of intolerable tension, of feeling so agitated and restless, and yet not knowing what to do to help them.

On October 20, under the guidance of Nellie Sengupta, the then president of the All India Women's Conference (AIWC) Chittagong Branch, the women of Chittagong formed a committee that would engage in relief work and for the recovery and rescue of the abducted women. From October 26 onwards, every seven days, this group went into the villages of Noakhali to investigate about the abducted women, undertook general relief work in the railway stations and listened to the descriptions of horror from the humiliated villagers. They prepared a list of the affected villages.

Mahatmaji reached Chamuhani on November 7. We approached him for guidance because we had not been successful despite our efforts. Sucheta Kriplani from Duttapara, Renuka Roy from Calcutta, and many more women workers of the AIWC and other organisations from different districts were gathered at Chamuhani. We sat together with Mahatmaji and with his guidance came up with a plan of action. We decided first of all to allocate a worker who would cover a particular police station. Her work would cover all the villages under its jurisdiction. Thus she would acquaint herself with the actual situation in the area and be able to find out about the abducted women. This was my first meeting with the Mahatma.

Following Mahatmaji's guidance, we started working at the Lakshmipur police station (PS). For about a month we examined the various problems of the people of these desolate, burnt and plundered villages. Alongside, we also assessed the extent of damage. Food, clothes and medicines were distributed. But when the villagers were called upon to return to their villages, they refused. On whose assurance would they return? Would they be safe? Meanwhile, Gandhiji had changed his plans. He camped alone at Srirampora village, Ramgunj PS. He called for volunteers who would be able to live in these isolated villages. He told us, 'It is at your assurance that the villagers will come back.' Gandhiji's fellow workers spread out into the different villages. But how could I go and live in the villages? I had my family, my children, the youngest of whom was still very small. I could not risk taking her with me and exposing her to the dangerous situation in the villages.

I wanted to keep my little daughter with me so that I did not feel compelled to return in a hurry. My husband told me, 'There is no hesitation on my part as far as you are concerned. But to take the little girl with you will affect your work and you will also be very worried.' I answered, 'As it is you are burdened all day with your work. You must take care of the two older children too. If I leave the little one here, at night you will spend sleepless hours looking after her. She will be missing her mother. This will be a source of tremendous strain. So let her come with me and stay with me.' Ultimately, after discussing the matter with Gandhiji, it was decided that my daughter would come with me. But I was not permitted to go home. Whenever my husband got a little time during the holidays, he visited our camp. At times he would come with social workers like Sanjibprasad Sen from Chittagong to visit Thakkar Bapa's camp in Char Ruhita.[27]

Our interview with Gandhiji before we went to Tumchar village has been well documented in Nirmal Kumar Bose's[28] writings and my husband's reminiscences.[29] I would like to state here what Gandhiji's directions were. He told us:

> We must ourselves go and live in the villages. Before urging the villagers to return, we must show them the way. We must live in

---

[27] A.V. Thakkar Bapa, General Secretary of Harijan Sevak Sangh, and a member of Gandhiji's team at Noakhali.
[28] Nirmal Kumar Bose, *My Days with Gandhi* (Delhi: Orient Longman, 1953, reprinted 1999).
[29] See pp. 54-62.

> these villages with our small children and be prepared to face any situation even if it is dangerous. If you are not prepared for this, then you cannot ask the villagers to return. You will have to be their source of strength and courage. Till you are successful in your mission there cannot be any talk of return. Therefore, think carefully before you decide to come forward for the work.

Phullarani Das (wife of Professor Ranendra Kumar Das) and I explained to Gandhiji that we had come to him after much deliberation and thought. Gandhiji then explained to us the future course of action and the various problems that we might face in these villages. He told us:

> Learn to love human beings. Do not harbour any malice in your minds. Work fearlessly and mix well with the villagers. Stick to the path of truth, only then can you hope for success, else you will be disappointed. If any one of you lives in the villages with fear then the villagers will realise that these people are scared.

He said:

> You will go to the villages deserted by their inhabitants. Seeing you, they should have the strength to come back to their villages. You should go to villages where the inhabitants are all Harijans. They are still living there with broken spirits. You will have to save them from the fear and despair that has enveloped their lives. Many of them have said that they were not tortured or hurt. But I know that is not true.

The Mahatma went on:

> Times are extremely difficult. I had imagined a very frightening and difficult situation. But the present crisis at Noakhali has surpassed my imagination. I hope that this terrifying situation will change very soon. But we must prepare ourselves. Only the future will tell us which turn the events will take. I still hope that life will

> return to normal, the nightmare of the riots will be wiped out, Muslims in general will change their minds and attitude. Until the simmering ash of the fire has settled and until we achieve some degree of success in our endeavour, I will not leave Noakhali.
>
> People say that my coming to Noakhali has created the problem. That is not true. I came here because there was a problem. You must know that the events of Noakhali were casting a dark shadow on India's future. But, however difficult the path seems, I will not be without hope. I will hope for peace and amity.

At that time we did not understand what Gandhiji meant when he said that the events of Noakhali are 'casting a shadow over the future of India'. In those days we could never dream or foresee that India would one day be divided. But a visionary like Gandhiji was perhaps able to see what lay ahead and must have been in deep despair. If he were alive today he would have been even more shocked and distressed by the present condition of the country.

I arrived in Chandpur on October 30. On the same night, I attended to a labour case on the station platform. The refugee woman who had come from Raipura Police Station (PS, Dist Noakhali) by a country boat was in great pain and was about to give birth. The RWAC (Royal Women's Auxiliary Corps) volunteers and the Red Cross Centre removed her promptly at my request, first to their room and then by jeep to Elgin Hospital where she was confined immediately. After this incident, I had talks with two groups of refugees: one from Raipura consisting of 60 men, women and children, and the other from Begumganj PS near Noakhali. The Raipura people were completely helpless. The Begumganj group, not altogether destitute, was proceeding to Muzaffarpur. The condition of the refugees at Chandpur station was simply appalling. The station master, station staff, the RWAC and above all the Red Cross were doing all they could under the circumstances. I slept in a railway coach provided very kindly by the Red Cross. Next day I attended a meeting of the Relief Co-ordination Committee at the Sub-Divisional Officer's bungalow. I explained my special mission to the SDO and Major Littleboy, who

Ashoka Gupta in Noakhali

was in charge of the military operation at Chandpur. I told them clearly that I wanted to see for myself the living conditions and mental state of the people after mass conversion, and specially to enquire as far as possible about the abduction and forcible marriage of women and young girls. Both promised to cooperate and help as much possible. Then I requested the major to keep his Military Police (MP) in check. I had witnessed the night before their rude and unsympathetic behaviour towards the refugees. At first he was a bit ruffled, but later on he calmed down and I found a very good friend in him during my short stay at Chandpur. He promised to talk to his MP. I did not know whether my requests resulted in any improvement. Later in the day, I visited some of the relief centres and talked to representatives of various relief organisations.

On the morning of November 1, I proceeded to Raiganj via Faridganj in a military launch kindly placed at my disposal by the Major. Early in the afternoon, we reached Faridganj PS (Tipperah Dist) and the relief camp there. Faridganj was a small place with insanitary conditions. There was a military post and an RWAC centre. There were about 5,000 to 6,000 refugees. They all complained of the bad quality of rice and said they suffered from digestive problems. As we had stopped there for a short time, I had no opportunity to visit any of the surrounding villages. I made a special point of asking some of them about abduction but could not get any definite information. One and all complained of the breaking of *sankhas* (the white shell bangles that married women wore) and the wiping of *sindur*. Quite a number admitted they had been converted.

By the evening we reached Raipura. On the way we saw only two homes burnt down. Devastation was not widespread, at least so it seemed from the launch. At Raipura, we put up at the two-storey house of the Pal family, which stood undamaged. But the family temple was completely dismantled and its furniture broken. The house was deserted, only a few employees of the merchant remained. The army was stationed in the house. The next morning (November 2), I went around the Raipura market and surrounding homes and met and talked to the local people. The market, which was very big, was almost deserted, as a high percentage of shops and stalls belonged to Hindus. Two big *akhras* (places of assembly of lower-caste Vaishnavs for worship and ritual singing) with their deities and belongings were completely destroyed and looted. Two huge mansions, consisting of several semi-detached houses within a few yards of the PS, were burnt down. One of these families was given shelter by a Muslim neighbour, at the risk of his own safety, for three days. Now this family was living in some temporary sheds constructed on their own plinth. Here also I got no news of abduction. They told me that there was talk of forcible marriage but it ended in talk only. Until the army was posted in the village all the males were made to go to the mosque for namaz. There was some attempt by the local Muslims to give them relief, but as soon as the army arrived relief was stopped and they were not called to the mosque for prayers.

Later in the morning, we proceeded in country boats towards Ramganj PS. After some distance, we got out of the boats and proceeded on foot. The first village we passed through had the name Karoa or Karpa—No 5 Union. Here mass conversion was complete and houses were torched. Men, women and children ran out to meet us and the women began to cry. All of them were eager that the army should be posted there or at least patrol the area at short intervals. I collected some burnt pages of the *Gita* and some handwritten *Chandipaath*. The next village was Chandipur—a Hindu majority village—very rich and fertile but devastated. Some families were still living here somehow. The army had been posted and there was a refugee centre, sheltering about 4,000 people. Mr R Gupta visited the village on November 3. RWAC was opening a medical centre soon.

By 4 p.m. we reached Ramganj PS after walking six to seven miles. At Ramganj there were about 10,000 to 12,000 refugees and even more were continually pouring in. Ramganj was a big place and conditions were better there than at Faridganj but still there was a limit to its capacity. There was a military post and an RWAC centre. On November 2, R Gupta went towards Dasghara to investigate. About 300 refugees followed him to Ramganj. Though he had an armed Inspector of Police and several armed guards with him, his party was attacked thrice by a big crowd. According to the inspector, whom I met the next day, they had to fire on the mob repeatedly and approximately 30 hooligans were killed.

We proceeded to Lamchar on the afternoon of November 3 and reached the village in about two hours time. Barring three big *pucca* buildings almost all other houses had been burnt down. These people had very bravely defended themselves with whatever they had and there was no conversion here. Two or three young men risked their lives and came to Ramganj to inform the police station and get armed help. They lay hidden in mud and water during the day and took two days to reach Ramganj. Lamchar village was lucky enough to get armed help the day after the terrible incident in Karpara at Rai Saheb Rajendralal Roy's house.[30] There were three refugee camps in the three undamaged houses sheltering two to three thousand people. There was a military post in the village and an RWAC centre was to open within a day or two.

Later in the afternoon we visited the scene of devastation at Karpara, which had perhaps no parallel. Rai Saheb's house, a big well-

[30] Rajendralal Roy, zamindar, had trusted his Muslim tenants who were peasants. When the latter attacked his house, he came down to talk to them. They beheaded him and then impaled his head on a spear and brandished it in the village.

built *pucca* building, was completely destroyed. The big rafters were reduced to charcoal. What happened here is well known. Four women related to the family had been abducted and had not yet been traced. One of them was seven months' pregnant, and another was a young girl aged about eight. A young married girl of a neighbouring family was also missing and as yet untraced. This information was given to me by reliable people. We later drew up lists of names of young women and girls, as young as nine, who were abducted, molested or forcibly married, giving as much detail as possible. Some of them were restored to their families.

Three hours before we visited Karpara, there was an attack on a party of refugees who were going to Lamchar with military escort and 25 volunteers. The military had to open fire twice: once at 12.30 and later at 2 p.m. When we were passing Karpara on our way to Lamchar we did not notice the attack or the shooting because of the dense vegetation. I talked to the police inspector and the subedar at Lamchar who had fired the shots. Karpara remained totally unprotected and its people were in grave danger.

We returned to Ramganj in the evening and proceeded to Hajiganj the same night. No more incidents occurred.

The pressing needs were:

(i) Search parties for abducted women.
(ii) Forming volunteer corps, patrolling areas with armed guards.
(iii) Posting of more military personnel.
(iv) Reassuring people that they are still Hindus.
(v) Reestablishing them in their own homesteads by putting up huts as soon as possible.
(vi) Making arrangements for reaping the aman crop[31] immediately and giving it to the rightful owners.

The concluding part of this essay is on pp. 96-7

[31] The paddy crop harvested in November-December.

Extracts from the Noakhali Diaries of Ashoka Gupta[32]

We are walking along the roads of Noakhali. The forested path is densely shaded. At the relief camp, we ran into an old man. We found him sitting on the porch of a house that had been reduced to cinders, a blank look in his eyes, infinite exhaustion and despondency on his face. I went up to him and asked how he was doing.

He could not answer me. Words are failing him; his voice is choked. There's an endless sea of tears behind the look in his eyes that are afflicted with grief. He handed me instead a document, three handwritten pages—a reply, composed in rhyme, to the question that I had asked him:

We were Hindus, but they turned us into Muslims. We were
dead yet alive, the Hindus of Noakhali.
We lost our faith, we lost our work, we lost everything. For what
sin were our temples burnt to ashes.
We have no abode of our own—they have been turned into ash,
piles of ash, a fantastic sight,
No one will quite believe it unless they see this place.
Much there was, much was lost, much did come to an end.
Noakhali became empty
of Hindu households, who knows where they went,
fearing for their lives, fleeing the country,
Some half-burnt, fled afar, others fled with their lives,
any where they could.
When we recall our sorrows our hearts burn with grief,
the fire that snatched children
from the mothers' arms. The mother says, weeping,
'Come to my arms forever,'
Keeps weeping and saying, 'Come, my dear child, come to me,'
Until she gives up on her life.
We are singed, we are burning, in the fire of our grief,

[32] This handwritten diary has not been published. No date is given at the head of the first entry. One assumes that this was written during the earliest part of Ashoka Gupta's visit to Noakhali in October 1946, a few days after the riots.

Chandrashekhar has no mother to mourn him.
His happy household is shattered, only the crematorium is left
for him now.
He gave away his wealth, they took away his wealth.
He gave up his daughter to the villains at last.
He begged for his life, but nobody heard his pain,
the cry of his soul,
Like a beast they tied him up. The flag of
misery flew high in the sky.

Chandrashekhar's wife, O brother, so innocent, so faithful she
was, like a daughter of the moon,
She too was burnt in the flames of grief for her husband.
By and by, such mayhem was unleashed on her house.
So many lives were sacrificed, so much turned upside down,
the heads of children slashed.
Everything's turned upside down.
Now, like a mendicant, she wanders around,
her body starving, stupefied.
She broke her conch-shell bangles, wiped the vermilion
off her forehead. Noakhali won't keep the Hindu women.
Their conch-shell bangles broken, the vermilion rubbed off their
foreheads, finally the men take them away,
Force them to read the kalma*, they want justice for the killings.*
Women kidnapped, women raped, women tortured, the earth
cannot bear the burden of this sorrow.
The fields will drown, the sins weigh down the earth,
The more the earth makes us weep, the more it will weep itself,
O how much shall we weep.
Only the poisoned tree will bear fruit, till generations last.
The fruits of one's labour will not go to waste, if the scriptures
are true, if faith remains unshaken,
Justice will surely be done.
What has happened, what is happening, what is to happen—fear

grips our hearts from time to time.
Like thunder it makes us tremble, hits us like a bolt from the blue.
Not a morsel in our stomachs now, not a scrap on our bodies,
where shall we go now?
Trailing this accursed luck? Who will feed us now with the love
of a mother?
With no land beneath our feet, we lie on the earth, and drink
water from an earthen pot.

Now we live in a house of sorrow, and speak of sorrow,
since we are here to suffer sorrow.
A night wasted in sorrow—let no one reprimand us,
for we are here to pay with this sorrow.
They have burnt our houses down, looted all that we ever had,
We get a poa *of rice at the day's end to keep ourselves going.*
But even if we get some rice, not every day do we get vegetables
to go with it,
There is no money left to buy even salt. We have kept ourselves
alive with our own lives.
We have not a scrap, nothing, nothing at all, tell us where
we should go?
Tell us what, O what, should we eat twice a day, we have
become so utterly bankrupt.
When they set my house on fire, the sight was unbearable,
At that moment, in my heart, I felt I'd be murdered.
I keened and wept,
When they tied up my hands, I pleaded with them,
fell at their feet crying,
Some told this old man, 'What's the point of weeping?'
I have already been released.
Not a morsel in my stomach, with nothing to wear, how,
O how, shall I survive this bitter cold?
I need a sweater, a blanket, for which I have come a-begging.
When I earned my freedom, I went everywhere,

looked inside out,
I took refuge in Upendra asylum, and then
I went away to Lakshmipur.

Who could have written a more detailed description than this one? Our journey resumed. We don't have permission to go deeper, into the interiors, yet we kept walking.

There is no end in sight. Since the last week of October, we have been going from one village to another, with some of the people of these villages who have joined us. They just wish to see how much damage has been done, how the houses have burnt in the fire and things have been looted so that people are unable to stay in these villages anymore. They besiege us with pitiful pleas, 'Come and see, just this once, why we were forced to desert our homes.'

We are left speechless. We too have come to survey the situation, we want to help them return to their villages and settle back in again.

They come from Gopinathpur, from Bamchandi, from Mojupur, from Parvati Nagar. The Debnaths are settled all over this area. There is a loom in every house. They earn their living by weaving. All stocks of thread, the paraphernalia of weaving, and the looms have been burnt to ashes. They have *pucca* houses, but these too have been burnt down. With their wives and children, the men have fled to the relief camp in the school building in Lakshmipur. Jugi Palli is absolutely empty.

We understand that it will be difficult to estimate the extent of the losses. It won't do unless we sit down quietly, work hard at it, and just carry on surveying the damage. Yet the news has reached us that Gandhiji will apparently be reaching Chandpur on November 7. On the same evening he will reach Chaumohani. In most of the villages, workers gathered their things and set out for Chandpur. I went to Chattogram for a couple of days, fetched the boys and girls to give them a Gandhi *darshan*, and reached Chandpur on November 6. The *darshan* took place as well. After a discussion of the working methods to be followed at Chaumohani, I set out with Phullarani Das and a few others to work for a longer period of time in the Lakshmipur region. And so, a diary of that period started taking shape.

November 8, 1946

At 9 in the morning we reached Lakshmipur from Chaumohani with one soldier and two volunteers. It was almost ten by the time we went into the village with six soldiers, one volunteer and two local men. First, we saw two burnt houses in Banchhanagar on our way past the village. We heard there was no one left in the village. Then came four-five Hindu houses on the way to Mojupur. In Aurangzebpur, we saw a house burnt and a few others lying in ruins. We were told that all the Hindus in this village had fled. Then we went to a Muslim house in Angilpur. There we saw two burnt rooms. They said that on the day of Id, the Hindus had set their house on fire. A little further ahead, we found that many people had fled with their possessions from the village of Sanarpur towards Lakshmipur. They had been forcibly converted to Islam. The conch-shell bangles worn by married women have been shattered, the vermilion on their heads has been rubbed off. They are of the Nath caste. So why are they fleeing now if such things were being done to them for so long? When we asked them, they informed us that the Muslims threaten them in various ways. Apparently, they set their own houses on fire, then put the blame on the Hindu boys, and take them away. We met Jagabandhu Debnath of Parvati Nagar. In his village too, everyone has been forcibly converted to Islam, houses have been burnt and looted. Then we went to the house of Jogesh Chakraborty and to see the Thakurs of Gourinagar. There is just one Hindu family left here. Earlier, there were two more. They have fled. The one that is left is petrified. But apparently the Muslims next door protect them. All their things have been looted. From there, we went to Ahladinagar, where all the inhabitants are Jugis. On the way, we saw many preparing to flee with their possessions, either on foot or by boat. We told them, 'There's such a lovely harvest in the village. If you leave now, all of it will be looted. And anyway, what will you eat once you leave?' On hearing this, they seemed to find some strength. Some even returned to Ahladinagar. We went to Radhamohan Nath's house. He is a well-off and influential man of this village. His *pucca* house has been burnt down. All the people of this village and about five hundred others from the adjoining village have taken shelter in his house. They are all extremely terrified. All of them have been converted to Islam. Some of them have been re-married to their husbands for this purpose. Even an old woman of 55 has not been spared. They are forsaking this abundant crop of paddy, betel-nut, coconut, and everything else, including their own homes—'What can we do?' they say. They were asked not to abandon this bounty of paddy, betel-nut and coconut. They were warned that there would be endless suffering if they left their village. They should live in big cluster, if they are feeling scared. Once they leave, they won't be able ever to return again. They seemed to find strength in our words. They said, 'Nobody has spoken to us this way so far.' Four houses were marked out. In each, 500 people will be living together.

Then we went to the house of Radhamohan Nath of Ahmednagar. He, too, is a well-off householder. His house has been looted as well. His temple has been razed. A centre was opened at this house. There are many Muslim well-wishers in this village. We went to the house of one of them, called Nabab Ali. We found the people of his family extremely upset by these incidents. On our way back, we went to Krishnadulal Nath's house in Parvati Nagar. All the Hindus of the village and some Muslim well-wishers had gathered there. The Hindus said that their well-wisher friends have really helped them a lot. One Hindu has been taken away for setting a house on fire. But he has done no such thing. One of the Muslims was ready to bear witness on his behalf. Many of the Hindus know the Muslims who have tortured them. But they do not feel brave enough to depose against them at the police station, lest the torture starts again. Having seen thus far, we started on our way back towards Lakshmipur.

November 9

First, we proceeded to the East, keeping Sahapur on one side and Banchhanagar on the other. Around that area, the big hospital of the Naths in Sahapur had been looted, and the house of the Acharyas in Sahapur had been reduced to cinders. From both places the Hindus have fled. Then came Mandalpur, where the Hindus have never lived. On the left bank, Parvati Nagar, on the right, Iyarpur. There are no Hindu inhabitants in these two villages. Then we went to the village of Khilbaichha. On the way comes Pal Bazaar. We met a man called

Abdul Matin in this village. He asked us, with some curiosity, who we were. Three hundred people live here. At present, there are no Hindus. Keeping Gopinathpur and Hetompur on either side, we kept going ahead. Here, half the population is Hindu and the rest Muslim. At present very few Hindus are left. Then we reached South Hasbadi, where three Hindus have been arrested for setting Mujilullah's shop on fire. They are Jogindra, Indrachandra and Pran Gopal of the Saha family. After we had crossed Ananda Saha's burnt house in South Hasbadi, a man from Bijoynagar told us that in Lakshmipur that Asiruddin, of Namaz Ali's family, has been stealing betel-nut and coconut from the house of Jagatchandra Balaichandra Majumdar. They are too scared to say anything. As a result, many of them are simply running away. Then, we met Nurujjaman Chowdhury, the president of Union number 1, in Kalir Bazaar in Bijoynagar. He informed us that the total population of the village is 1,700 of which half are Hindu, and that nine houses have been burnt down. We met someone from Bijoynagar while we were on our way to Itipur. We met the postmaster on our way to Hasnadi. He was asked to fetch his family from Bijoynagar. Then, leaving behind Bharat Dhupi's burnt house, on the way to Hasnadi, we met Mujafar Islam of the Punjab regiment 7/15. We met many Muslims. Asking them to gather in Bhuniya's Haat, we went to the house of another Nath, Gurudas Kabiraj. 324 Hindus in all live in Hasnadi. 102 in Panchbari, of whom about 20-22 are left at present. Three of the houses have not been looted or burnt, but the prayer rooms have been defiled, cows slaughtered, and the faith has been insulted. The Muslims had deposed in retaliation on the 5th and the 6th, leading to a mass exodus from the village on the 8th. On the 5th and the 6th, after the shop right in front of Haoladar and Sayyed Ahmad Khan's Dar-ul-Azaan were burnt, many Hindus were arrested. Of late, the Muslims had been very helpful. Now people said that in Mirjapur, two cousins—a brother and a sister—were converted to Islam and married off to each other.

Narabhuniya's Haat. Some Hindus and Muslims were gathered here. Among them, two old Muslim men, Abdul Rashid and Rasool, assured the Hindus, saying, 'We have protected them each and every day, and will continue to do so.' But not all the people's attitude seemed cordial.

We were told that there are 200 Red Cross volunteers here. We met Captain Abdul (his father's name is Ismail Byapari), who comes from West Hasnadi. The Hindus informed us in confidence that this man has carried out forced conversions, broken conch-shell bangles worn by married Hindu women, and done much else. Half a mile north of Bhuniya's Haat lay Mirjapur. There are 200 Hindus there, belonging to the washerman caste, Naths and Namashudras. Everyone has been forced to convert to Islam. We left the house of the head washerman of Mirjapur, Ishwarchandra Das, at around 1.30 in the afternoon, and reached the house of Bijoynagar's postmaster at 2 p.m. There has been looting here, a thousand rupees have been extracted as donation for the (Muslim) League. We found a wound on Harimohan Chakraborty's mother's throat. She got it when her *kanthi*, a kind of a necklace, was cut off. We found that Chandramohan Nath's fingers have been cut off. Ramanimohan Das was taken away against his wish and asked to set Muslim houses on fire. He managed to flee somehow. At three in the afternoon, we reached Bholanath Saha's house in East Chandi. Very little has been looted from the house. People have been forced to convert. Nurul Islam and a few others are being threatened by some of their Muslim neighbours for protecting the Hindus. Then we passed by the burnt houses of Jogen Saha and some others and reached the house of Krishnashundar Kabiraj of Hetampur through South Hasjadi. Here Muslims and Hindus from Hetampur, Jahanabad and Hasnabad had gathered. They haven't been looted and their houses haven't been burnt down. But donations for the League have been extracted from everyone. 500 people live in these three villages, of which 100 are Hindu.

There is terrible fear among the Hindus. After 30-40 Hindus were arrested on 20 charges brought against them, many have fled from their villages. The Hindus don't feel brave enough to speak out in the streets, to give depositions, or to name the criminals. It is unlikely that they will ever depose against their tormentors, if they wish to continue living in their villages.

We met McInerney, the District Magistrate of Noakhali. We discussed the barbarity and inhumanity that are being carried out in the name of Red Cross operations. It was asked whether it is necessary to deploy 1,900 volunteers for relief work. Dr Guha and Abdul Hakim of the Social Service League had a heated debate over the irregularities that are being carried out in the name of the Red Cross. We met the Deputy Superintendent of Police and the circle officers. We also met Heramba Bhattacharya. We learnt that finally all the Hindu detainees have been granted bail.

November 10

First, we went to Dalal Bazaar at 9 in the morning. The remains of the house of Nalinikishore Roy, the zamindar of Dalalbari, were lying about. We saw Dalaldighi on the way. From the state of his house we could guess the amount of preparation that had gone into the attack. We met people from Gazipur and North-South Haschadi in front of this house. Not all their houses have been burnt. But all of them have fled or left their homes in fear. Here the Muslims took away Haridasi, the 17/18-year-old daughter of Krishna Saha, son of Panchkari. Her previous husband was called Mahendrakumar Saha, both her paternal home and the house of her in-laws are in Gazipur, in the north and the west, respectively. The girl was found a day later. Three days after Lakshmi Puja, as the police went into the village, everyone fled to Lakshmipur. The Muslims continue to threaten Pyarimohan Saha of Haschadi. At Mahaprabhu's place we ran into people from Haschadi, South Haschadi and Gopinathpur. Here, one man had been tied up and burnt to death because he had dared to defy the mob. Five people have died in Dalal Bazaar. Two groups have clashed with each other at Kapalituli. As a result, the Hindus have been variously hurt and wounded. There are 2,000 Muslims in Kapalituli, and 200-300 Hindus. In the village of North Haschadi, 11-year-old Surbala—daughter of Bisakha (whose father is Gourchandra Nath) and Nandalal Nath, who lives with his in-laws—was coerced to marry a Muslim man from the village. When the girl refused the proposal, her uncle was tied up on the evening of November 6, and Sona Miyan's house was set on fire. On their part, the Muslims surrounded their house. The women fled in fear. Then Jagadulla Bhuniya's son, Kala Miyan, asked Bisakha where the household goods were. 'The looters have arrived,' he said, 'I will protect everything.' When the looters reached, they found nothing in the house. So they became suspicious of Kala Miyan. They tried to force Radharani, widow of Nabakumar, the eldest son of Ras Gobinda Jugi of North Haschadi, to marry a Muslim. But she has managed to flee somehow. They tried many times to force Kanchanmala, widow of Sudhindrakumar Das of South Haschadi, to marry a Muslim. She has managed to escape by the skin of her teeth. Yet on the other hand, Kalachand Goswami of Dalal Bazaar told us that his house had been spared only because Becha Sardar, Bandhan Ali and Aan Miyan had intervened. On the way to Charmandal, in front of the mosque with the open cannon, we met Ishan Ali, son of Akram Ali, of the 25 Bihar Regiment, and another soldier, Sona Miyan, son of Ali Salimuddin of West Lakshmipur. Both of them said that they were going home. We reached Charmandal at noon.

Noon, Charmandal. The inhabitants of Charmandal all belong to the Namashudra caste. The number is almost 6,000. Most of the houses have been burnt down. Almost everyone has remained in the village. First, the house of Ramesh Das. In this house, 17 quarters have been burnt, a hundred people live here. We heard in this house that Satish Das's wife, Bishnupriya, has fled in fear to Lakshmipur after the Muslims came and tried to force her to marry one of them. Afterwards in Charmandal, all the Namashudras had gathered at the house of Haralal Roy. Here we heard that they had tried to force married women, widows and others, to remarry. They had also tried to marry off Muslim girls into this family. We learnt that the Muslims keep saying that neither the military nor the volunteers would be around forever. 'Your fate ultimately rests in our hands,' they say. They take away coconuts and betel-nuts from their trees, cut paddy from their fields, raise objections to courtyards being plastered with cowdung, and to women ululating.

Gopal and Ramgopal have been threatened that if they bear witness against the Muslims they will be cut into pieces. Lakshmi Pyne's wife, Saraswati Sundari (60), was beaten with a stick and had her money and jewellery taken away. Brinda Majhi's wife, Manadasundari, and daughter, Malatisundari, are Tuka Miyan's accomplices; they helped him stir trouble. Malatisundari has been staying with Tuka Miyan for two years. Jogindra Haldar's daughter, Pramila, was tortured in the back garden during the riots. Here Anil Das, son of Bhairav Das, was severely injured. He has recovered now. Purna Das's son Gopal drowned in the water. Another girl here has been beaten up as well.

At 2.15 p.m. we went to Rajani Haldar's house in Charruhita.

1. Aushya Miyan (Ashal Ali), son of Karim Bux, had held a sickle at the throat of Rajani Halder's married daughter, Karunya (12/13 years old), and forced her to remarry. The ceremony was conducted by Maulabi Ahmadullah. The girl's aunt and mother were also taken away along with her. People from her home went to fetch her twice. Three days later, when they went to get her again, she was allowed to go home. At present, the girl is with her husband, Ananga Majumdar, in Noakhali.
2. Sudhanya Majhi's 10/11-year-old daughter, Abala, was married off to Tayeb Ali's son, Anu Miyan (15/16 years old). She was taken away that night but returned home the following day. Her parents and the rest of the family have been threatened.
3. Jamshed Ali's son, Majidullah, had come to marry Kamini Majumdar's daughter, Karunya. After much difficulty, Bhagaban Chandra Majumdar could stop the wedding by quoting the Sarda Act. For this reason, the girl's uncle, Gaganchandra Majumdar, was stabbed in the ear. Bhagaban Majumdar was struck with a stick.
4. Mahendra Haldar's wife, Bidhumukhi, tried to get Sachindra Haoladar's daughter, Jogomaya, married to Abdul's son, Animullah, but didn't succeed.
5. A married woman, Nanibala, was solicited for marriage by Sona Miyan's son, Muhammad, and Gunamani (26), a widow, was asked to take Balla Bhuniya as her husband. Nanibala has fled to her husband's home and Gunamani to her sister's.
6. Bapi Miyan wants to marry Bhagaban Pandit's daughter, Shishubala. Currently, she has gone off to stay with her husband.
7. On our way back, we heard Radhanath Sarkar's daughter Nirmala (9/10 years) was married off to Manu Miyan, son of Jalal Ahamed, on the 27th day of Ashwin. In Charruhita, where the girl's current in-laws live, 125 houses have been burnt. But all the people have stayed back in the village. They are all Namashudras.

In Charlamchi, we found the houses of Khagendra, Abhaycharan, Purnachandra, Shyamacharan Sardar, Kamini Kumar Mistri, Sashimohan Mistri reduced to ashes. All the inhabitants remain there.

We saw the burnt houses of Radhagovinda Sen and Sachindra Kar of Banchhanagar. There we ran into Basana Dutta, a female vaccinator.

November 11

At 11 in the morning, we went through Samshurabad Lamchabi of the Number 4 Union. On the way, we came across a volunteer called Amanullah, wearing a Red Cross badge. The corps captain of that volunteer group is Captain Jainul Abedin. Volunteers: Hindus 5, Muslims 45. There are 12 members in the joint committee: 1 Hindu and 11 Muslims. The population of the village: Hindus 150, Muslims 1,550. This village has not been looted, its houses have not been set on fire, and the Muslims here have not unleashed anarchy. The miscreants had come close to the village but did not get in.

Then we took the boat, keeping Shakchar on the right and Tumchar on the left. On the right, we saw the burnt remains of Nalinibabu's courthouse in Shakchar. We reached Tumchar at noon. We rested awhile at the house of Pareshchandra and Saratchandra Poddar. Two school-going Muslim boys joined us. One of them is Abdul Gani Miyan's son, Lutfar Rahman. The population of the village: Muslims 5,000, Hindus 2,000. The one Hindu family that is living in Shakchar came along as well. On Tuesday, the 28th of Ashwin, trouble erupted here. On Monday the 27th there was trouble in Charruhita and Charmandal. In Tumchar, 11 of the 28 houses have been burnt. In this house, they have slaughtered a cow, cooked it, and force-fed it to the residents. The prayer rooms of all the houses have been defiled.

Marriages

1. Sarat Poddar's unmarried daughter, Bindhyabasini (10), was forcibly married off to Mojubani (17/18), son of Palla Miyan, a resident of Maulabi Hajibari in Charruhita. They held a sickle at the girl's father's throat, forced him to read the *kalma*, and give the girl away in marriage. The girl's father and a few others from the village went along with the girl to her in-laws. The girl's aunt lives in Charruhita.

After much pleading, the girl's father and aunt could manage to bring her back in the evening. They had put *mehendi* on the girl's hands and a *tuti* around her neck. It's being said that they will take away the girl again. The girl has been asked to eat beef. They have even thrown raw beef at her. The girl's father has been told that now that they have been converted to a good religion, they will surely attain salvation.

2. Surendra Karmakar's daughter, Parulbala (11), was forcibly married off. It is suspected that one of Hatiya Kaji's men had wanted to marry her. Nura Chora, *aka* Nuru Miyan, suspects Gonu Miyan. Here, they dangled a sickle around the girl's head and asked everyone to take Allah's name.
3. Manitara (12/13), father's name Chandrakanta Talukdar. Her mother is no more, she has a stepmother. On the 28th day of Ashwin, she was taken away to Munshibari to get married. Her father and relatives went along with her. She has been married off to Majid Ali's son, Labja Miyan. The in-laws want to take the girl in, and give her clothes and jewellery. But the girl's family hasn't agreed. They will not let the girl go unless they are given a *kamin* deed. The *maulabi* said that he would arrange for it later. But after the troubles were over, they came and took back the clothes and jewellery.
4. They want Prasanna Talukdar's daughter Karunya (10/11) to marry Jitu Miyan's son, who is 12/13 years old.
5. Habibullah of Charruhita wants to marry Bhagaban Majumdar's unmarried daughter, Kusumbala. He goes to the village with this intention. When the girl's father and others in the village plead with him desperately, falling at his feet, he leaves without marrying the girl.
6. Habibullah wanted to take Kamini Majumdar's unmarried daughter, Makhanbala, to his own village and marry her. She was saved when her next-door neighbours arrived on the spot.
7. They had wanted to get Rammohan Mistri's unmarried daughters, Kusumpriya (10), and Monopriya (12), married. The men were not at home. Villagers suspect that it was Habibullah who had planned this.

8. They wanted to take away Kalidas Poddar's daughter, a widow named Shishubala.

We went to Purnachandra Talukdar's house. It has not been burnt. Here we meet a few Muslims from the village—ex-chairman Mohammad Miyan, Renu Miyan (secretary of the joint committee), Ayub Ali Chowdhury (*talukdar*), the schoolmaster, Abdul Jabbar, who is an MA. He is married and calls himself a member of the Congress. He has helped the Hindus a lot. Here we met Anima Das, who was injured in Tumchar.

Habibullah wants to take Girish Talukdar's daughter, Swarnamoyi, to Charruhita to get her married there. We heard here that there are 25 volunteers in Tumchar. Hindus 3: Satindra Karmakar, Gadhadhar Majumdar and Rebati Talukdar. One can't get people to cut the harvest in Tumchar. The Muslims don't buy betel-nut here.

9. Then we went to Rajkumar Majumdar's house in Dasgram. In this house, 10/15 rooms have been burnt. A little bit of the paddy has been cut. People are too scared to go and work in the fields.

Iyadullah and Abdul Chhamant Munshi and Machhlanda Maulabi had proposed marriage to Khagendra Majumdar's daughter, Menaka (12). Hearing this, the Majumdars went absconding. All three looted the house and set it on fire. We heard that for the past two-three days, Muslims have been going around telling everyone that they suspect that the men of the village were returning home disguised in women's clothing. Then we went to Patari House. Six rooms have been burnt here.

Someone from Charruhita wants to marry Sudhakanta's daughter, Trinayani (10). Upendra Das's wife, Anasuya, told us that when she was hiding in Korban Ali's garden, Nur Miyan's wife had told her, 'Why do you flee? You should become our relatives instead. Eat *gosht* with us every day, get your daughters married into our families.' When Anasuya tried to sprinkle water on herself, Nur Miyan's wife called out to someone and said, 'Make our sister (*beyan*, referring to the mother-in-law of one's son or daughter) a *paan*.' Korban Ali had told Bhabatosh Das, 'If you want to hide in my garden, you will have to pay me.' Das took out the money that he had kept tied to his waist and handed it over.

Dr Gofur Ali proposed marriage to Bhupendra Das's daughters, Shakuntala and Kirtibala.

The weddings of Brajamohan Das's daughter, Pranpriya (11), and Parvati Das's daughter, Haripriya, were scheduled at 10 o' clock that day. The weddings could not take place because the military managed to reach Lakshmipur in time.

Sudhakar Das's eligible daughter, Nayantara (14), was abducted by Nura Chor, taken to Charruhita, and harassed.

Pankajbala, a married girl of 17/18, was taken to the garden and tortured. When her mother-in-law passed away they did not let the corpse be cremated. Finally, the corpse had to be set afloat in the river.

On our way to Banikanta Das's house we crossed Kalikanta Haramohan Das's place. Gonu and Runu Miyan had pleaded with Banikanta Das's daughters, Niru and Minu, to marry them. When they refused, their house was burnt down.

In Dasgram. Volunteers: Muslims 25, Hindus 9. We left behind Poddar House and went and sat in Umed Ali Byapari's house. Here we met his grandson, who is a volunteer captain. Umed Ali Byapari said that the Das family was not at home. If they had stayed on, their house would not have been set on fire. We had gone to settle the matter amicably, but since there was no one there, nothing could be done. We heard reports that this man is a good sort. On the way, we stopped at the bailiffs' and the boatmen's.

In Dasgram, all the houses have been burnt except for Talukdar's place. Here, little boys have shattered the conch-shell bangles on the wrists of married women and rubbed the vermilion off their foreheads. Donations for the League have not been extracted in Tumchar and Dasgram.

Translated by Somak Ghoshal from the manuscript diaries

Letters

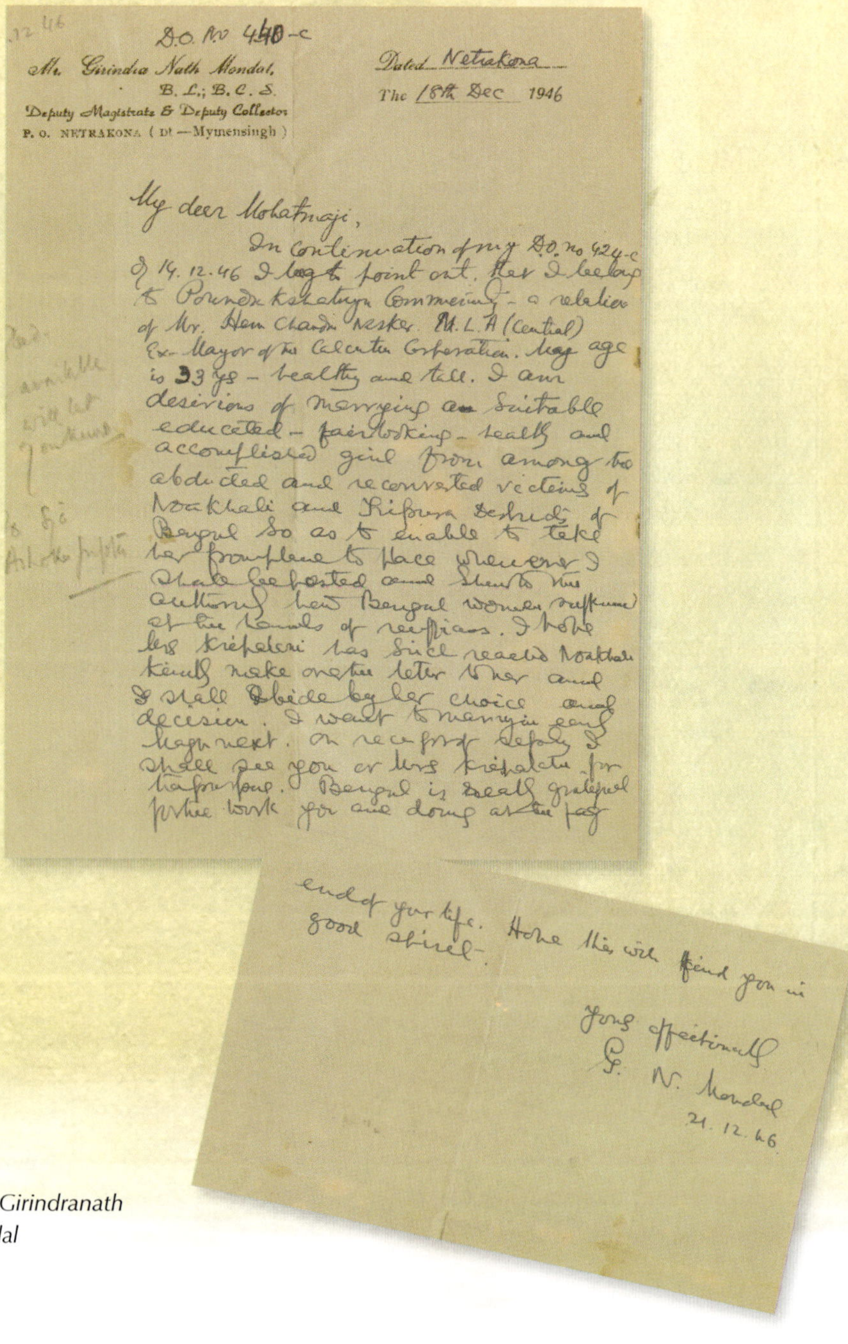

D.O. No 440-c

Mr. Girindra Nath Mondal, B.L.; B.C.S.
Deputy Magistrate & Deputy Collector
P. O. NETRAKONA (Dt.—Mymensingh)

Dated Netrakona
The 18th Dec 1946

My dear Mahatmaji,

In continuation of my D.O. no 424-C of 14.12.46 I beg to point out that I belong to Poundra Kshatriya Community - a relation of Mr. Hem Chandra Naskar M.L.A (Central) Ex-Mayor of the Calcutta Corporation. My age is 33 yrs - healthy and tall. I am desirous of marrying a suitable educated - fairlooking - healthy and accomplished girl from among the abducted and reconverted victims of Noakhali and Tripura districts of Bengal so as to enable to take her from place to place wherever I shall be posted and show to the authority how Bengal women suffered at the hands of ruffians. I hope Mrs Kripalani has since reached Noakhali. Kindly make over the letter to her and I shall abide by her choice and decision. I want to marry in early Magh next. On receipt of reply I shall see you or Mrs Kripalani for the purpose. Bengal is really grateful for the work you are doing at the fag end of your life. Hope this will find you in good spirit.

Yours affectionately
G. N. Mondal
21.12.46

From Girindranath Mondal

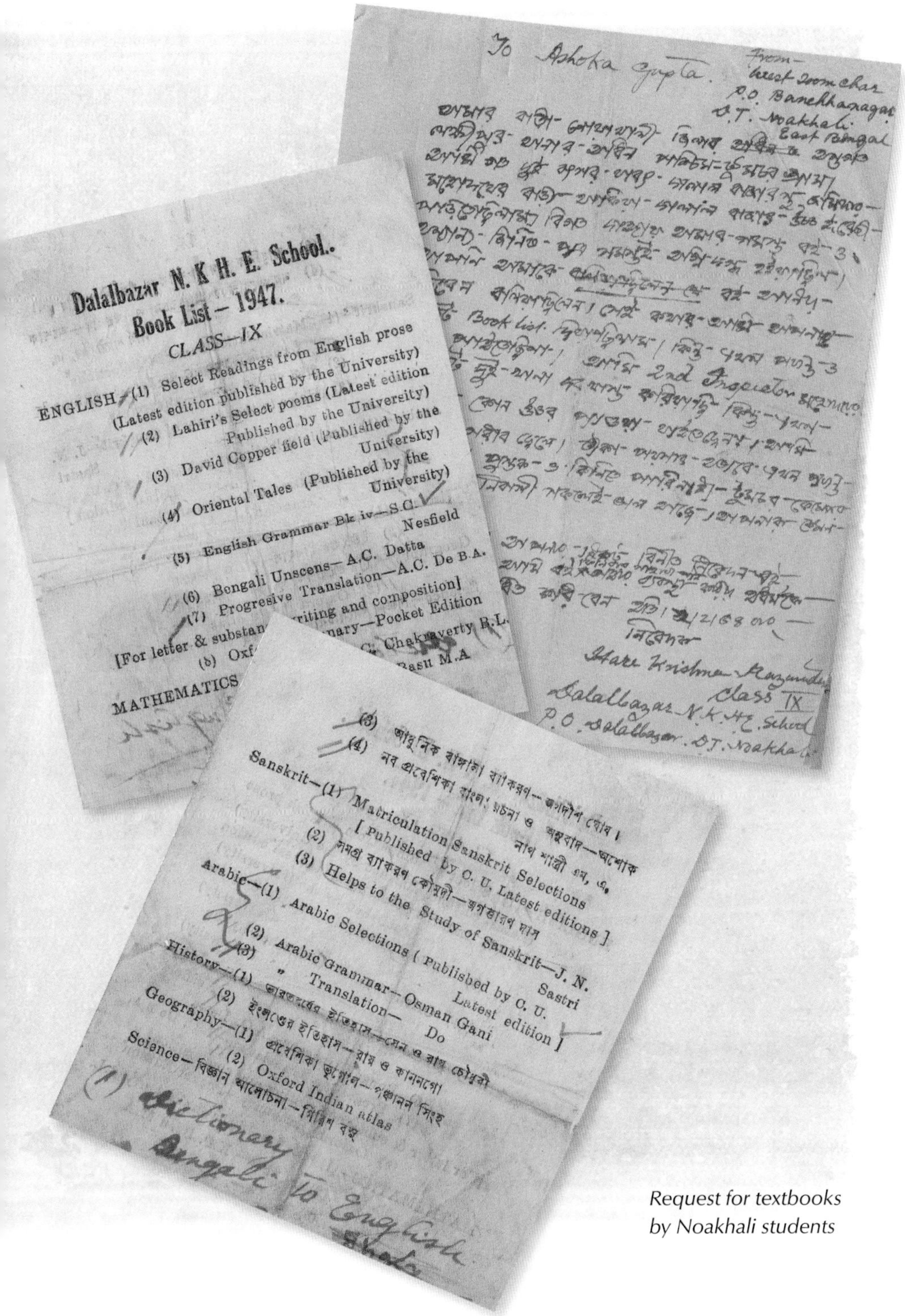

Request for textbooks by Noakhali students

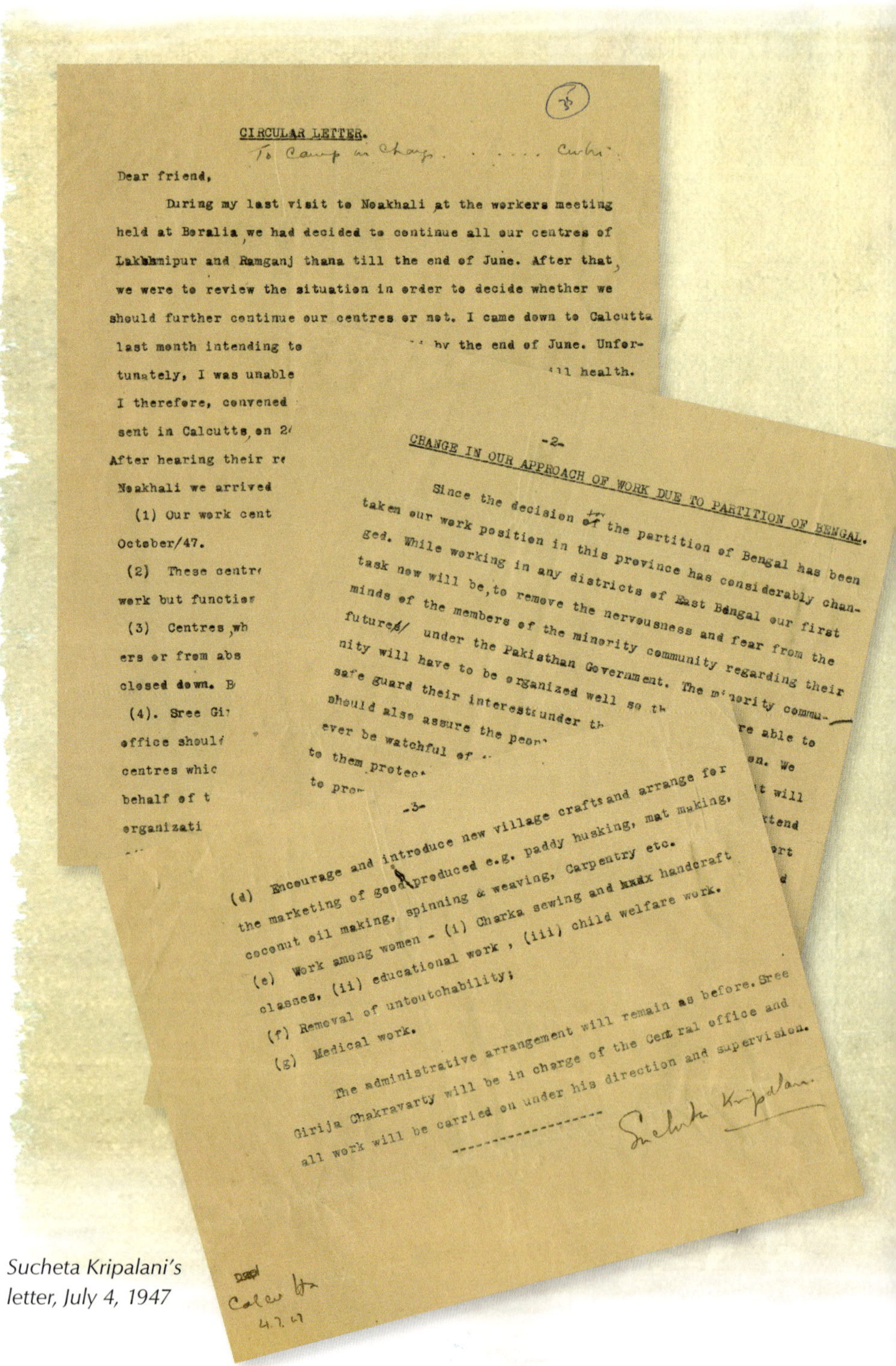

CIRCULAR LETTER.

To Camp in Charge . . . . . Cuchi.

Dear friend,

During my last visit to Noakhali at the workers meeting held at Boralia, we had decided to continue all our centres of Lakshmipur and Ramganj thana till the end of June. After that, we were to review the situation in order to decide whether we should further continue our centres or not. I came down to Calcutta last month intending to ... by the end of June. Unfortunately, I was unable ... ill health. I therefore, convened ... sent in Calcutta, on 2... After hearing their r... Noakhali we arrived ...

(1) Our work cent... October/47.

(2) These centr... work but functio...

(3) Centres, wh... ers or from abs... closed down. B...

(4). Sree Gi... office shoul... centres whic... behalf of t... organizati...

-2-

CHANGE IN OUR APPROACH OF WORK DUE TO PARTITION OF BENGAL.

Since the decision of the partition of Bengal has been taken our work position in this province has considerably changed. While working in any districts of East Bengal our first task now will be, to remove the nervousness and fear from the minds of the members of the minority community regarding their future under the Pakisthan Government. The minority community will have to be organized well so th... safe guard their interests under th... re able to should also assure the peop... en. We ever be watchful of ... t will to them protec... tend to pro... rt

-3-

(d) Encourage and introduce new village crafts and arrange for the marketing of goods produced e.g. paddy husking, mat making, coconut oil making, spinning & weaving, Carpentry etc.

(e) Work among women - (i) Charka sewing and handcraft classes, (ii) educational work, (iii) child welfare work.

(f) Removal of untouchability;

(g) Medical work.

The administrative arrangement will remain as before. Sree Girija Chakravarty will be in charge of the Central office and all work will be carried on under his direction and supervision.

Sucheta Kripalani

Calcutta
4.7.47

Sucheta Kripalani's letter, July 4, 1947

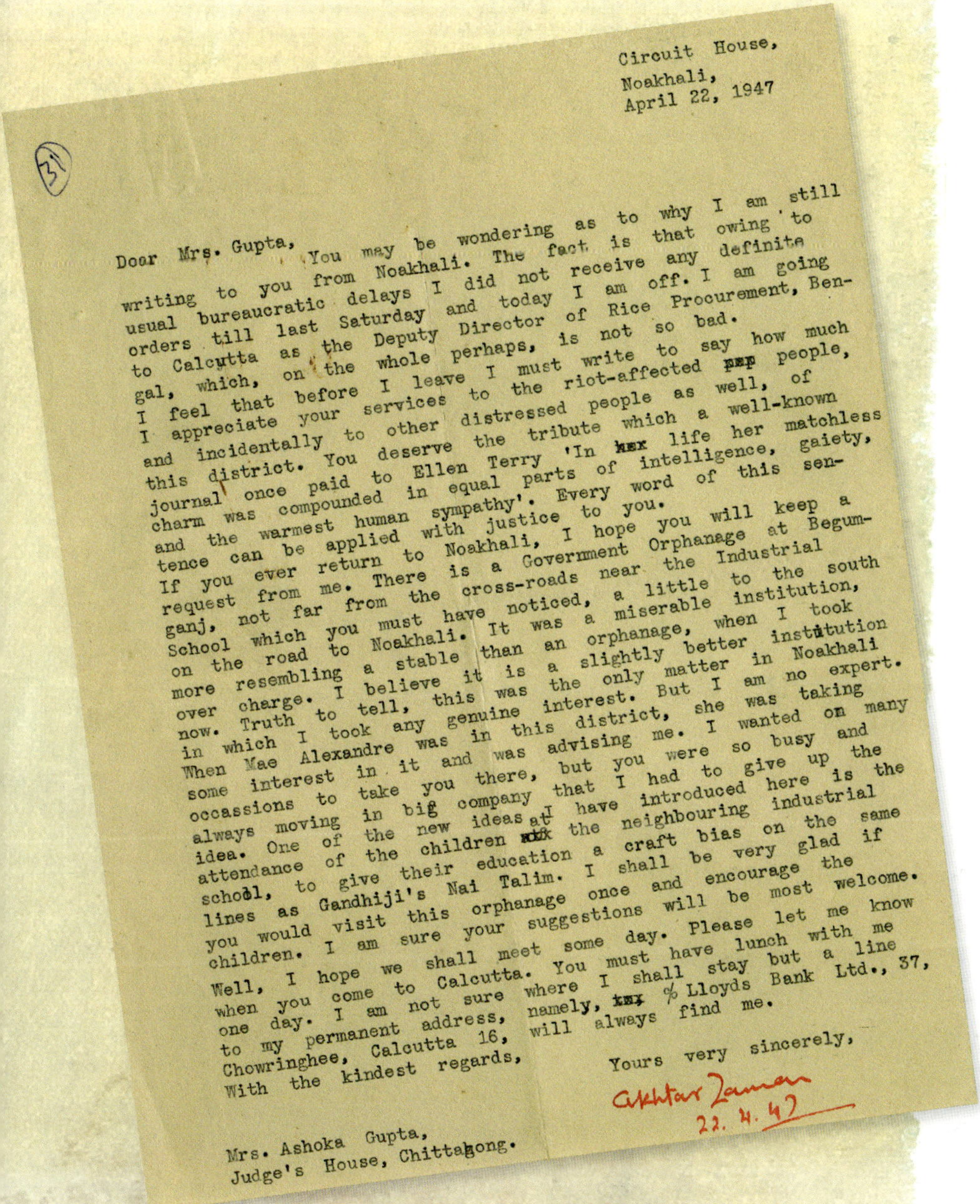

Circuit House,
Noakhali,
April 22, 1947

Dear Mrs. Gupta,

You may be wondering as to why I am still writing to you from Noakhali. The fact is that owing to usual bureaucratic delays I did not receive any definite orders till last Saturday and today I am off. I am going to Calcutta as the Deputy Director of Rice Procurement, Bengal, which, on the whole perhaps, is not so bad.

I feel that before I leave I must write to say how much I appreciate your services to the riot-affected people, and incidentally to other distressed people as well, of this district. You deserve the tribute which a well-known journal once paid to Ellen Terry 'In life her matchless charm was compounded in equal parts of intelligence, gaiety, and the warmest human sympathy'. Every word of this sentence can be applied with justice to you.

If you ever return to Noakhali, I hope you will keep a request from me. There is a Government Orphanage at Begumganj, not far from the cross-roads near the Industrial School which you must have noticed, a little to the south on the road to Noakhali. It was a miserable institution more resembling a stable than an orphanage, when I took over charge. I believe it is a slightly better institution now. Truth to tell, this was the only matter in Noakhali in which I took any genuine interest. But I am no expert. When Mae Alexandre was in this district, she was taking some interest in it and was advising me. I wanted on many occassions to take you there, but you were so busy and always moving in big company that I had to give up the idea. One of the new ideas I have introduced here is the attendance of the children at the neighbouring industrial school, to give their education a craft bias on the same lines as Gandhiji's Nai Talim. I shall be very glad if you would visit this orphanage once and encourage the children. I am sure your suggestions will be most welcome.

Well, I hope we shall meet some day. Please let me know when you come to Calcutta. You must have lunch with me one day. I am not sure where I shall stay but a line to my permanent address, namely, % Lloyds Bank Ltd., 37, Chowringhee, Calcutta 16, will always find me.

With the kindest regards,

Yours very sincerely,
Akhtar Zaman
22. 4. 47

Mrs. Ashoka Gupta,
Judge's House, Chittagong.

From Akhtar Zaman

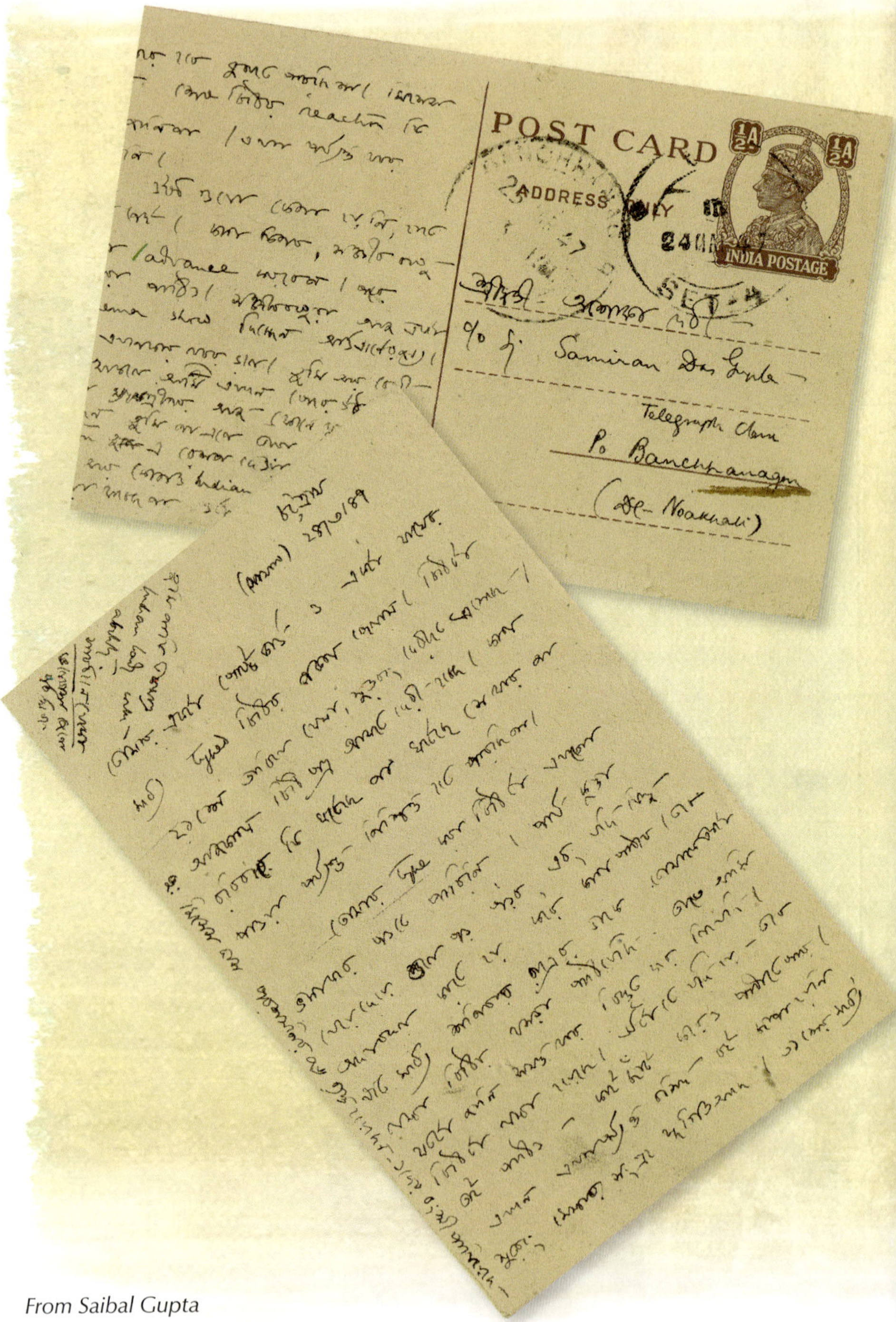

From Saibal Gupta

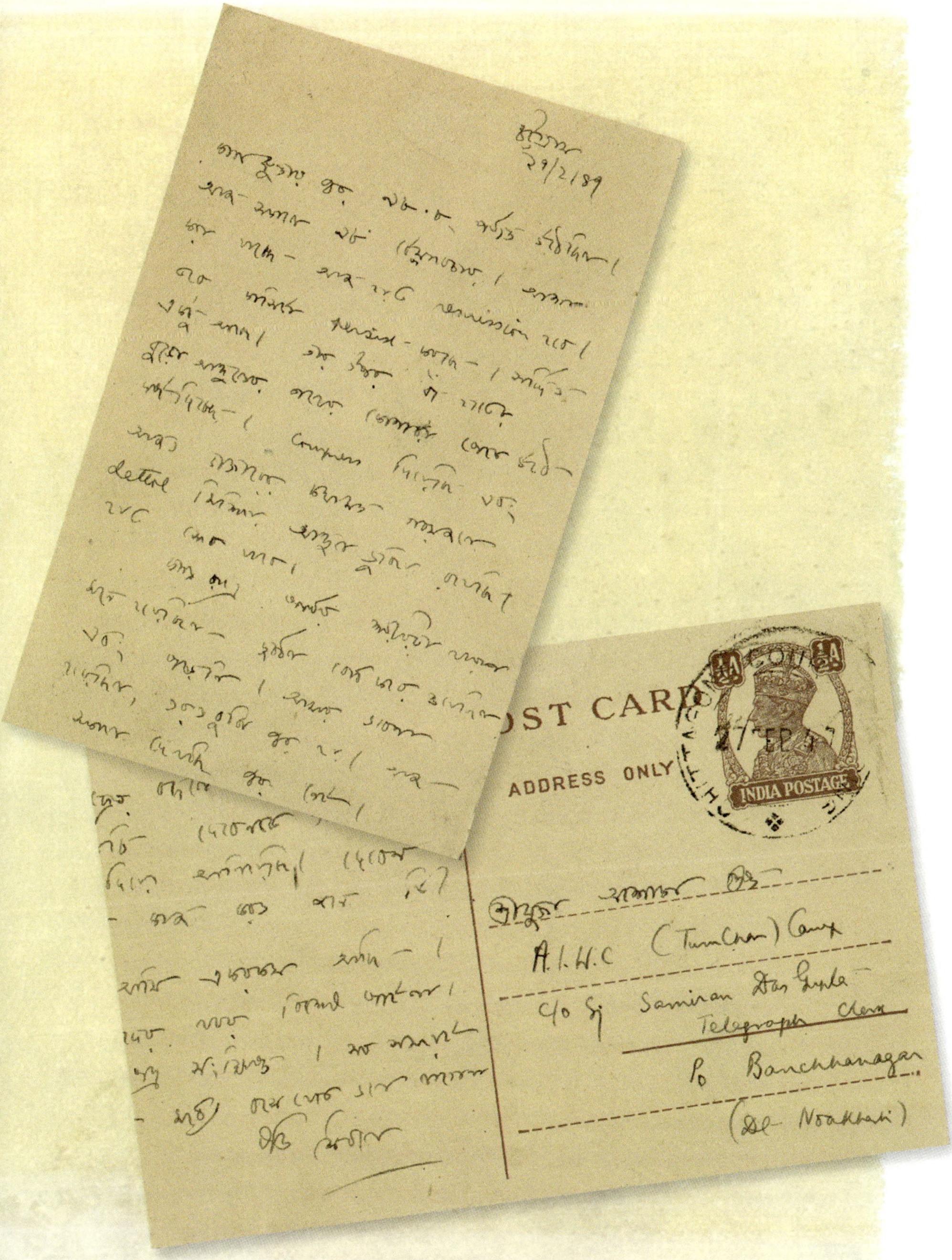

From Saibal Gupta

Letters of Saibal and Ashoka

Saibal to Ashoka

Srijukta Ashoka Gupta
AIWC (Tumchar) Camp, C/o Sj Samiran Dasgupta
Telegraph Clerk, PO Banchhanagar
Dt Noakhali, Chattogram
January 29, 1947

I am writing on this official letterhead as I cannot seem to find any other paper. So, who knows, this may end up sounding like an official letter!

We had to face a few problems on the way from Lakshmipur to Chowmuhani. First we had a tyre puncture, then we had to pump air into the tyres; also, the radiator was leaking, so we had to stop every now and then to take water. So, by the time we reached, the bus that had left after us had already reached. There were a couple of times when we had been scared that we might be left stranded on the road. Anyway, the one good thing about my taking the earlier bus was that you could leave for Tumchar a little earlier. If I had waited for the next bus, you would have got delayed.

I went to Jogenbabu's house and contacted his younger brother, Upenbabu, and the Relief Officer, Sukhamoybabu. I have arranged for the bundles of clothes to be sent. They will probably reach Rambabu's house in Lakshmipur tomorrow (30/1/47). They will have to be picked up from there. Jogenbabu had asked me to eat at his place, but I only had tea with *payesh* and *pathisapta*. Kunta too did the same. Neither of us was hungry. I met Dhiren Dutta and Bibha Mitra there; they were both heading for Kolkata after hearing that their children were unwell. Kunta slept well in Laksham. We didn't have any trouble catching the CTG Mail. There was an almost empty compartment, so both Kunta and I had a good sleep on the way. We reached this morning. I had to call home and have the car sent to us.

Partha is fine. Do not worry about him; I will take good care to make sure he doesn't feel depressed. My impression of him on my return was quite positive. But he was saying, 'Why didn't you get Ma?' He had one of the green coconuts sent by you that very morning. He will have the other one later. Kunta told him, 'Ma has sent you this as a bribe.' She remembered what I had said and applied it in the right place! A few days ago, the Muslim League descended on Partha's school and forced the students to go home—Partha returned home before the car could go to the station to get him. Many communist leaders spoke at their Manimela meeting on the occasion of Independence Day* on Monday. The same thing recurred at the Jatramohan Sen Hall that evening when Partha and his friends went to the Brahmo Mandir for the *Balak Balika Sammelan,* the gathering of young boys and girls. Partha was present on both occasions. There is no problem with exposing oneself to all points of view and then deciding for oneself what is right and what is not; rather, there is much to be gained from it. Still, I am not sure if they are old enough for that. Partha came back and recited a large chunk of Kalpataru Sengupta's speech; of course, he also said that many of the boys in his class were upset because of the overt anti-Congress sentiments in his speech...

Take care. And don't <u>overwork</u>. There is something intoxicating about humanitarian work. It is only natural that the *approval* one earns from oneself and from others would nudge one to exert oneself even more—this is so true of you. That is what makes me worry about you. Do not think that I have exorcised my doubts just because I have gone and inspected your circumstances. There are enough problems there. I hope Mrs Kanjilal has reached today. The teacher, whom all of you praised so much, was a great disappointment for me. Rather, the common villager is more inspiring for me—at least, he does not wear his education like a burden weighing him down.

Love. Do not neglect Kasturi.

Yours,
Saibal

*Before 1947, nationalists observed January 26 as 'Independence Day'.

February 17, 1947

Kunta's temperature had climbed to 98.8 yesterday. It was 98 this morning. I think we can expect *remission* today. The fever has been persisting, though. She has a bit of a cold as well. Moreover, the nail of her left thumb has got infected and is giving her a lot of pain. I have used a compress and I am getting her to dip her thumb in warm water mixed with Dettol as per the doctor's advice. It should be okay.

Partha seemed unwell last night—he was feeling weak and lay down and could not study. I was worried lest he, too, should catch the fever. But he isn't running a temperature today, thankfully.

I have brought Deben, to replace Mahendra. Do you have any idea what kind of a worker Deben was?

I am doing all right. I don't get much news from you. Only a few brief letters. I hate spending all my time indoors like this.

Yours,
Saibal

Ashoka to Saibal

Tumchar
March 3, 1947

I have not been able to write to you these last few days. I posted a letter the day I left for Hawimchar. I reached the very next day, but I was so tired I could not write to you. So I missed the post yesterday. I am writing to you today, but this letter, too, will be only a brief one.

You are worried, but I have been worried, too—because I did not receive any letter from you for two consecutive days, and also because Kunta had fever. I did get Sanjibbabu's letters, but without your letters, I remain worried and unhappy. I did not write because I was expecting your letter—I thought I would then respond to what you had written. I did not get any letter from you; so I, too, did not write.

Kasturi is fine. She had a couple of sores but they have almost healed. Mrs Kanjilal's sons are not well. The camp has been well and truly set up now.

Baba, my Baba, Kunta and *dada*, come here.[33]

Kasturi is really disturbing me! She is not letting me write. Such a long time she spent struggling with the pen—she said she wanted to write to you. You can see the result. She says every day now, 'Won't we go to Baba?' If I say, 'No,' she says 'Yes.' And she spent almost the whole of day before yesterday crying for Kunta. And every time there is a song, she clamours for Parthasarathi. She sings a lot these days.

You all will leave on the night of the 6th and will reach here on the 7th. It will probably be around 11 a.m. when you reach. I won't go back to Lakshmipur unless some other work comes up. I will have someone wait for you at the bus stand. Once they see you, they will go up and help with the luggage. If you don't see anyone at the bus stand, leave your luggage with Samiranbabu at the post office and move on. You don't need to bring much in any case. There are beds here, a couple of mattresses and three pillows—you only need to bring one more. If you are afraid it may be cold on the way, you can carry a blanket though it is quite warm here now. Another bottle of methylated spirit would be nice, but don't go to too much trouble for it—we are managing fine.

Hope you all are well and will be on your way without any hitches on the 6th.

Love.
Yours,
Ashoka

All the manuscript letters translated by Sayantan Dasgupta

[33] This is written in a child's handwriting. It is probably a line penned by little Kasturi in the middle of the letter being written by her mother.

Our Last Days in Noakhali Before Partition

Gandhiji was not in favour of partitioning India. In the last prayer meeting held on February 28, 1947, in Haimchar, Comilla, on his way to Bihar, he told us that he would like to come back to Noakhali to complete the task he had undertaken: the cause of Hindu-Muslim amity. His four-month stay in that part of East Bengal which had witnessed the mad days of loot, arson, conversion and killing of peaceful neighbours was coming to a close. The next morning he was proceeding to the riot-affected areas of Bihar where communal frenzy had taken its toll of innocent lives in the Muslim community. One could see that he was deeply moved and grieved. He felt that his physical presence in Bihar at that moment would halt the madness for retaliation and restore peace, and ultimately good sense would gain ground. He hoped that we would carry on with the task entrusted to us and would not leave our work in Noakhali at that stage. Scores of workers like us, who remained in Noakhali in those days to spread Gandhiji's message of love and peace and worked for the rehabilitation of the utterly destitute people who had lost their hearth and home, were faced with a challenge. With him there, it had been easy. His promise to return to Noakhali was a great source of encouragement for us.

But the restoration of peace in Bihar was followed by a series of riots in Punjab and the country was facing a terrible crisis. Gandhiji moved from Bihar to Delhi. His prayer meeting message remained unheeded. In the affected areas people ignored the appeal for a change of heart. Nobody was willing to listen to the lone voice of Gandhiji. The situation was going from bad to worse as the decision to partition the country was about to be announced. We in Noakhali were shocked to hear the declaration on June 3, 1947, over the radio. Naturally, we were not prepared for such a drastic decision. We faced a situation when all the work done during the past few months in restoring communal harmony was shattered by the declaration to partition the country. Our workers were heartbroken! The subsequent history is known to all of us, but nobody could visualise or predict the endless migrations on such a massive scale from both ends of the same country where the two communities had lived side by side

Ashoka Gupta stands next to the Gandhi Smarak Samman awarded to her in 2007 for lifetime achievement. Gandhiji and Kasturba look on

for centuries. I can still hear the sad voice of Gandhiji telling us in Noakhali: 'It is like a bad dream—a nightmare. Unless you work hard, our Motherland will face a disastrous fate.'

From Jasodhara Bagchi and Subhoranjan Dasgupta (eds)
The Trauma and the Triumph
(Kolkata: Stree, 2003), pp. 159-167

Dandakaranya , 1963

In early August 1947Ashoka Gupta and her family left Chattogram for Kolkata, where she was able to meet Gandhiji. The migrations from East Pakistan continued...as described by Ashoka Gupta in this article, written in 1964.

Dandakaranya: The New Home of the Refugees

It is hardly necessary to recall the events that followed the partition of India in August 1947—which brought almost the entire Hindu and Sikh population of West Pakistan to this side of the border. The exodus was instantaneous. The refugees left their ancestral homes and villages so suddenly and so quickly, and under such difficult conditions accompanied with violence, that they could hardly bring with them even their personal belongings. Relief camps were opened where lakhs of displaced persons received free rations and clothing, free medical facilities and free education for their children until these refugees were gradually dispersed to their rehabilitation centres.

In the case of East Pakistan, the really big influx started from East Bengal only after the riots of 1950, and the refugees poured into India in a steady stream until 1957 when the new law of migration prevented the refugees from crossing the border without a migration certificate. By this time, according to government figures, over 40 lakhs of people had crossed the border from East Pakistan. Out of this huge population (according to government records), only 3.5 lakhs sought assistance from the government and were accommodated in various camps and Homes mostly in West Bengal.

This meant that only 10 per cent of the people who migrated from East Pakistan between 1950 and 1957 remained the responsibility of the Government of India, whereas the remaining 90 per cent settled themselves somehow, mostly in West Bengal and some in adjoining areas, especially in Assam. In 1958, all the camps in West Bengal were closed. By 1959, doles or subsidies were also stopped in all the camps and it was decided to disperse and rehabilitate all the 45,000 families who still crowded the camps and who were mostly agriculturists waiting to be rehabilitated on lands as promised by the authorities. The Government of India decided that 10,000 such families would be absorbed in West Bengal and the remaining 35,000 sent to the rehabilitation sites in other parts of the country. As there was no large tract of land available anywhere in India to accommodate such a large number of people, it was decided that the Dandakaranya forest area be developed, and the bulk of the refugees who were mostly agriculturists who had lost their land in East Pakistan, be resettled there.

The area of Dandakaranya is approximately 77,670 sq kms, spread between the districts of Koraput and Kalahandi in the state of Orissa and the district of Bastar in the state of Madhya Pradesh. Out of this area, the Dandakaranya Development Authority which was set up for this rehabilitation purpose was given by the respective states an area amounting to only 155,236 acres of land after releasing 25 per cent of developed land for the local people. This could accommodate about 7,000 displaced families, i.e., a population of approximately 32,000 people. Dandakaranya is a sparsely populated area and is not a vast empty tract of land. The population consists of adivasis and local people who have their agricultural lands between large tracts of forests and hills. Therefore when the new influx started pouring across the border of East Pakistan to West Bengal in 1964 and the Union Ministry decided that they should be sent over to Mana Camp, it created a hope that Dandakaranya would ultimately accommodate them all. This proved to be entirely unfounded because Dandakaranya, as I have already mentioned, had come to a saturation point by accommodating 6,874 families up to the end of October 1963. The distribution in the different zones was as follows:

Paralkote Zone (MP): 2,253 families
Pharasgaon (MP): 250 families
Umerkote (Orissa): 2,854 families

Malkangiri (Orissa): 1,023 families
Work Centre (Camps): 349 families
Working under various schemes: 145 families

Thus, the large number of refugees who had been sent direct from the East Pakistan border to Dandakaranya were really being kept temporarily in a transit centre at Mana, which is 9 miles off Raipur in the district of Raipur, Madhya Pradesh, and is 150 miles away from Dandakaranya region. It would not be correct to state that Mana is a part of Dandakaranya. It is only the railhead from where refugees have to enter Dandakaranya if they want to come via Madhya Pradesh. The other gate is Vizianagaram in Andhra Pradesh, which is 92 miles from Koraput and is another railhead for entry into Dandakaranya. Mana, once an army camp and abandoned after the last war, is a large treeless stretch of *morrum* land, unfit for agricultural purposes. Mana is extremely hot in summer. There is great dearth of water. The possibilities of subterranean water resources were yet to be explored when the new migrants began to arrive in an endless stream. There were two big halls at Mana which had previously belonged to the army and the new arrivals had only those halls to be accommodated in.

Social and Health Problems

The concentration of such a large number of families belonging to different walks of life in a small area raises many social and health problems. Under the existing system, these families are received at the Raipur Railway Station, brought in Project buses and trucks to Mana transit centre and to other transit centres which were opened recently in the vicinity. After their names and family details have been entered in the camp registers and preliminary medical check-ups, vaccination and inoculation have been done, they are either accommodated in tents or in semi-*pucca* bamboo huts. They are supplied with one cooked meal in the community kitchen on the day of arrival and given dry rations or a maintenance grant so as to enable them to make their own cooking arrangements. This method kept them busy immediately from their arrival for some time; but the problems stated above arise within a short period.

Among the new migrants who had arrived in the Mana transit camps were and are a considerable number of families who fall under the Permanent Liability category. Up to April 30, 1964, about 798 families without any adult male member had arrived and there were 105 families who were infirm, ill and disabled. There are also families who comprise old and weak parents with minor children. It is necessary to take special care of them and to start a home with facilities of primary schools, a hospital, a production-cum-training centre, creche, balwadi etc. Condensed courses for 100 adult women may also be set up in this home for unattached adult women. Some young able-bodied women who have some education can go in for training as nurses and *balsevika*s. Permanent Liability families with male members may also be screened out and sent to some of the homes already existing for such people, in West Bengal, Bihar (Betia) or Punjab. Single, old and aged men and women should be sent to religious places like the Banaras Home for the Old and Aged which was set up by the Ministry of Rehabilitation earlier, or their care can be entrusted to voluntary associations who have enough experience in this line.

Some Urgent Needs

Apart from these families who are in the Permanent Liability category, most of the families amongst the new migrants have three or four small children. The women in these families have hardly any time for taking training in crafts after standing in the queues for water, medical facilities and rations. Still there is a great demand amongst young girls from the age of 12 upwards for such training. If for each sizeable group of families one craft centre is started in the camps, in each specified area, it will be of immense help to the young mothers and daughters. Many boys and girls studying in secondary school should be given an opportunity to continue their studies. There is no such programme for them as yet.

There was only one hospital with 16 beds at Mana which has now been extended for 100 persons. The invalid diet was not up to expectation in the hospital in the beginning. There was at least one childbirth a day. Besides, there were many cases of advanced pregnancy in the antenatal list. The Project was hard pressed for children's clothing and baby sheets, as hardly any of the refugees who had crossed the border had a second set of clothing with them.

Assistance of Voluntary Agencies

In this context, the efforts of the non-official agencies and contribution for the welfare of the migrants were spontaneous and generous and need to be recorded, lest we forget them. The social welfare organisations started approaching the authorities from the very beginning, to find out in what manner they could serve the cause of distressed families. Organisations like Bharat Sevashram Sangha; Madhya Pradesh Christian Council; Indian Red Cross; Ramakrishna Mission; Missionaries of Charity from Calcutta; Bisthapit Sahayata Samity, Raipur; Municipal Committee, Raipur; Marwari Relief Society; Bharat Scouts and Guides, Raipur district and West Bengal State; Bhilai Mahila Samaj, 'Tridhara' from Bhilai; Kalibari Association, Raipur; All India Women's Conference, Calcutta Branch; Gandhi Smarak Nidhi; Family Planning Association, Raipur; Shantinagar Mahila Samity, Raipur, and many others from Raipur and Calcutta came forward and discussed, and planned how best they could help without their efforts overlapping.

The welfare work at Mana was then coordinated by the members of the Central Social Welfare Board and MP State Board who were present on the spot. The efforts of the above voluntary organisations and various other semi-government organisations, such as the MP Home Guards and the National Discipline Scheme were channelised with the approval of the authorities.

School Facilities

Primary schools consisting of 1,200 children were started, and secondary schools consisting of 78 children. Mother Teresa's organisation, Missionaries of Charity, offered the services of their nuns who were trained teachers. Balwadis consisting of 150 children were organised and run with the help of refugee girls by a Mukhya Sevika of the West Bengal State Social Welfare Advisory Board who was deputed by the Central Social Welfare Board. A hospital for convalescent children with 65 beds was organised by Dr Bhandari who was sent by the Indian Red Cross Society, at the instance of Dr Sushila Nayar, Union Health Minister and Chairman of the Indian Red Cross Society after her visit in April 1964. Miss Paul, Staff Nurse of Indian Red Cross Society, organised home nursing training for girls from displaced families. Twenty-four girls were successful and are doing very good work.

Medical and Nursing Care

Medical and nursing was taken up later on by Dr Miss Gertrude of Mother Teresa's group of nuns, belonging to the Missionaries of Charity who worked continuously for over a month to save the ailing children. The young women and girls amongst the displaced persons ungrudgingly drew scores of buckets of water, washed clothes, cooked invalid diet and kept the dormitory of the hospital clean. The Mukhya Sevika from Central Social Welfare Board did the night duties throughout this period and was made responsible for cooking and supplying invalid diet for these undernourished kids with the help of refugee women and girls from amongst the Permanent Liability category.

The children who underwent treatment in this ward during this six-week period were suffering mostly from the after-effects of measles in the form of broncho-pneumonia, dysentery and diarrhoea. There were also cases of acute malnutrition and rickets. Mumps also came in an epidemic form. It was a big challenge to the nuns and the staff to bring them back to normal conditions. The social workers, nuns, volunteers from amongst the refugees and the sevikas visited tents daily to pick up children who needed special care and diet. Smt A John Matthai, Chairman, Central Social Welfare Board, and Dr Soundaram Ramachandran, Union Deputy Minister for Education, visited the Mana Camp and held discussions with the authorities as to how the conditions could be improved, specially those of the sick and under-nourished children and women who had lost male members either at the border or during the riots.

Milk, bread, rice, *dal,* soup, barley, Horlicks, *chira* and multi-purpose food and hospital beds, bed-sheets, children's clothes etc,

Dandakaranya, 1963

were received from various charitable societies in Calcutta and Raipur. Special mention may be made of Bisthapit Sahayata Samity, AIWC Central Branch and Bharat Scouts and Guides.

Volunteer Corps

A volunteer corps consisting of 32 displaced girls was organised and trained as Girl Guides. They helped in distribution of clothes and gifts received through various donors, took patients to hospitals and mended, sorted and cleaned gifts of clothes, bottles and tins which were very often dirty.

Over fifty refugee girls joined craft classes where four sewing machines were constantly in use for providing uniforms to Balwadi children, girl guides and the Volunteer Corps. They also made rag-dolls and balls for the hospital children. Sewing machines were donated by Bhilai Mahila Samaj, Bisthapit Sahayata Samity, Family Planning Association of Raipur and Indian Red Cross Society.

Maternity and Child Welfare Centres were put in proper shape by Miss Paul of Indian Red Cross Society with the help of doctors and health visitors for the Project. All equipment for these centres was supplied by Bisthapit Sahayata Samity including bedding, bed sheets, and cots. Rubber sheets were supplied partly by Bata Waterproof Company and partly by others. The Trained Nurses Association of India contributed generally to equip the Maternity and Child Health (MCH) centres in the Mana group of camps.

Some cash donations were also received from various sources. The money had been spent on invalid diet in the convalescent children's hospital and MCH centre and by giving cash allowances to nurses and balwadi attendants who were recruited from amongst the refugee women as suggested by Dr Soundaram Ramachandran and Smt AJ Mattai. In addition to this, large consignments of clothes, old and new, and many other gifts were received and distributed to the displaced persons who came in pitiful conditions.

During the time of her visit to Mana, Dr Sushila Nayar brought 1,000 lbs of milk powder and arranged for further supply of powder from the Madhya Pradesh quota and USAID to the extent of 3 lakh pounds to the Project authorities for distribution amongst the displaced people. These are being distributed to over 4,000 children, nursing mothers and sick persons daily. Voluntary workers of the Central Social Welfare Board, Ramakrishna Mission and Madhya Pradesh Christian Council, and sevikas and teachers of the Project schools are helping in the distribution.

School tiffin supply of *chira, gur* and loaves was a regular feature in Mana. These were being supplied by Bharat Sevasram Sangha and Bisthapit Sahayata Samity. Multipurpose food which was supplied by Red Cross was very much appreciated by children, and multivitamin tablets have also gone a long way to improve their health.

It is difficult to assess what a family needs when it has left all its belongings behind, particularly when one does not have first-hand knowledge.

Many Needs of Inmates

Apart from clothes, old and new, which were donated by all associations in Raipur and Bhilai for Mana Camp inmates, it was found that they needed buckets to carry and store water. The Women's Coordinating Council, Calcutta, gave one each to most of them; but some who came via Hashnabad had none. Municipal Committee, Raipur, came forward and gave approximately 5,000 buckets. Washing soap was greatly in demand, as many of them had not had a proper bath for weeks. School children from Calcutta supplied soaps, matchboxes and candles through Bharat Scouts and Guides. Lanterns at night were the next need. Bisthapit Sahayata Samity and the MP Christian Council and Bharat Sevasram Sangha came forward to supply lanterns. Central Social Welfare Board sent Mukhya Sevikas who started balwadis and craft classes. Sewing machines, yarn and materials for craft classes were given by the Family Planning Association, Raipur, Bisthapit Sahayata Samity and Santinagar Mahila Samity and Red Cross Society. It was all a sincere cooperative effort to do good for the people who had to face sufferings of great magnitude.

When we consider the question of welfare services for the migrants from East Pakistan, we should bear in mind that these persons who have crossed the border and left their ancestral hearth and home behind are from various walks of life. Although the majority are farmers who owned sufficient land to maintain themselves and their family, there are people who belonged to various trades and professions and industries. In spite of the recurring phenomenon of riots and oppression in East Pakistan they had stayed on their lands and maintained their positions for 17 years, because it was profitable and they had deep attachment to the soil. By coming away, they have gained nothing, lost all they had and they are now fighting a losing battle by trying to prove that they were not idlers.

The Endless Quest

The crowds that we come across in camps are groups of exhausted, tired and baffled people. They have trekked a long way and they want now to settle down and strike root somewhere. They realise that this is a temporary phase—these transit camps, but they do not understand why some homestead plot should not be allotted to them which they can call their own and pay for in instalments, side by side with the provision of work, as is proposed now. It is said that they do not want to work and that most of them want cultivable land. For the agriculturists it is a natural desire, although we may not have enough land to spare for them. I have seen how, with the onset of the monsoon these people have cried for the land which they left behind and which may not be cultivated this season.

They have left all they had, but many families have carried bundles of seeds of all kinds in the hope of seeing a new life grow out of them. Wherever they have gone, be it in tents or bamboo shacks or hutments, a patch has been dug up in no time and they have sown some of these seeds. Men and women are hungry and eager for land where they can sow these seeds which they feel is their only asset, brought from their ancestral land. I have seen women work day and night for their families and for their tiny little households in tents, and then for their little kitchen garden.

Men, specially industrial labourers, have gone from place to place seeking work but there is enough work to go round. Refugee traders have set up bazaars in no time, but they have not enough money to establish themselves in trade. Professional people have registered themselves in employment exchanges and elsewhere, but there again are not enough jobs to go round.

Amongst the tribals, the Santhals, the Hajangs and the Chakmas—who have crossed to this side via West Bengal—are anxiously waiting for a plot of land which they can call home. They, like any other human being, wish to visualise a stable existence, not a nomadic life with no future and a hand-to-mouth existence working as day labourers at a minimum wage.

A well-planned rehabilitation programme with a sympathetic approach is awaited now, so that these uprooted people may regain a sense of security.

Published in *Social Welfare*,
Vol II, no 7, 1964

Note: A full account of the callous mismanagement of the Dandakaranya project can be found in Saibal Kumar Gupta's *Dandakaranya: A Survey of Rehabilitation* (Calcutta: Bibhasa, 1999).

With Social Welfare Board delegation, Cuttack, 1958

Ashoka Gupta consistently believed in the power of legislation to give Indian women opportunities they had never enjoyed before. This is seen in the next three articles, the first written while the constitutional framework of the new nation was being constructed, the second fifty years later, and the third, a talk given when she was herself in her 80s, reflects her concern with the problem of ageing citizens.

Women and Governance

I am going to discuss to what extent in the new (post-Independence) regime Indian women have acquired rights in elected bodies and in matters of governance. But to understand what is new in the new system we have to understand what our condition was under the old dispensation. Hence I feel we need to examine what rights women had before this new government took over.

We need not look a long way back. If we examine the progress that we have made in the 20th century itself we will get a perspective on the status of women within the nation and in their own communities.

Let us first discuss the rights that women have acquired with regard to the governance of the nation. These rights fall primarily into three groups. Firstly, according to the provisions of the Government of India Act of 1935, women could be elected to reserved seats in the legislative councils. For example, in the 250-member Bengal Legislative Council four women could be elected. However, there was no bar to their being elected to the general seats as well.

Those who paid taxes to the Union Board, Municipality or the District Board or paid income tax to the government were allowed to vote and elect representatives. In this respect it could be said that women had rights similar to that of men. However, as women usually did not have rights to property, very few women actually enjoyed voting rights.

Secondly, not all areas of work or earning a livelihood were open to women and even if women gradually acquired rights in some spheres, they did not have equal rights with men in the workforce in every field. Even if they did the same work, women were often not paid wages equal to that of the men. In many cases women labourers were given lower wages than men. Thirdly, women did not have the right to inherit their fathers' property; now, even after being granted equality under the Fundamental Rights of the Constitution, they do not have this right to property.[34] Consequently even in recent times women's rights to share in the governance of the nation were limited.

Apart from legal rights, if we analyse the condition of women in the last twenty years from the social perspective, it appears that firstly, even though there was no social taboo on girls' education, there were many ancillary difficulties. Those obstructions will remain unless education is made compulsory. Secondly, even though there are fewer cases of child marriage, the practice of getting girls married before the age of fourteen has not stopped altogether. In fact in rural areas it still happens with everyone's consent. It has not yet been possible to even raise the issue of divorce or other reformative changes. Our social consciousness is still undeveloped. Women are still trapped in and compelled to follow conventions, social prescriptions and customs even though these have not been constructed by them.

Considering the prevalent circumstances, under the new government women have acquired, almost without their asking or agitating for them, many fundamental rights which women in other countries have struggled hard to get. Yet it must be said, right at the beginning, that we need to understand whether the opportunities and legal rights that we have acquired with respect to nation-building are commensurate with our social opportunities and rights.

Under the government in the new nation, the first right that we have got is the right of citizenship or the right to vote. After getting this we felt that we would be able to select our representatives to the elected bodies according to our preference. Also that at the time of election

[34] This article appeared in 1953, three years prior to the passing of the Hindu Succession Act in 1956.

we will be able to vote according to our independent judgment and try to get a representative of our choice elected. This right applies to both men and women. Everyone above the age of twenty-one is eligible to vote. For us women, though, it is a new right that was not available to us before on such a large scale across classes. It does not need saying that the granting of this significant right has conferred on women an increased responsibility, and women must augment their awareness to be able to function according to the demands of this new responsibility.

Those days are gone when men said, 'You women, what do *you* understand', or women themselves said naively, 'What can we women say'. This is a very significant citizen's right that we have got quite effortlessly but its exercise is a grave responsibility. All women need to understand this very well. We have to ensure that those who are respected by virtue of their honesty, dedication and character, who are committed to the economic and cultural progress of the nation and who are aware of the fundamental rights of women, should be entrusted with the power to govern. This opportunity is now available to adult women along with adult men. It is only our ability to handle this opportunity judiciously that will reveal whether we deserve to be given this responsibility and right. We should not get carried away by the flow of events.

So far I have spoken about how as citizens we should elect our representatives to the Legislative Assembly. Now I would like to say something about the responsibilities and duties of those women who will be elected to the Assembly or Vidhan Sabha. I have already spoken about what the condition of women was like earlier in this century and the process by which they could get elected to the Vidhan Sabha. Like delicate Kabuli grapes swathed in cottonwool, two to four women would sit in the reserved seats in the Legislative Assemblies and Councils. Their opinions hardly counted in the framing of the Constitution or the laws. Now under the rights given to the people by the new government, the voters, if they so desire, can nominate women to all the seats and they can elect anyone they like. Hence, it would not be a problem if women in numbers greater than those who are already contesting the electoral battles (in the whole of India) came forward to contest; in fact it might be beneficial for women at large. It will be the responsibility of those who are elected to participate in the framing of laws and the governance of the country and all the work that would lead to development and the progress of the nation. I believe that I do not have to convince you with examples that there is no lack of such women who are capable by virtue of their education, commitment, capacity to work, strength of character and experience to take up this responsibility. People will readily acknowledge that great women like the late Sarojini Naidu, the late Sarala Devi Choudhurani, the respected Jyotirmoyi Ganguly, the brave Matangini Hazra and Pritilata Waddedar and, the youngest among them all, Purnima Banerjee, have all demonstrated their strength and character and made invaluable contributions to the progress of the nation. In the area of social service we remember with gratitude the contribution of the late Sarala Ray (Mrs PK Ray), Kumudini Basu and the Honourable Lady Abala Basu. It seems unlikely that there will be a scarcity of accomplished women in that same country, now independent, which in the past boasted of such great women in the areas of politics and social service. If you consider everything and take into account the position women and children ought to occupy in the new plans for the nation, then you will all realise that it is imperative to send capable women to Parliament and to provincial legislative assemblies.

Many would like to know how a woman assists in governance if she is elected to the Vidhan Sabha. Whoever is elected, be it a man or a woman, he or she could function as member of a party or independently. If he or she has been elected from the victorious party that will form the government, then he/she can express his/her opinion regarding the party policy on governance in the party forum. Sometimes the party changes its position to accommodate considered opinion on serious issues. Also, the elected representative could be selected for a position in the Cabinet. In that case one is dealing with government work at first hand. And if one is elected from a smaller party or as an independent candidate, then he/she can influence government policy during the framing of laws by proposing amendments or voting. This is how men and women intervene when elected by the people. Though the granting of rights on such a massive scale is new for Indian women, I have no hesitation in saying, and I say it proudly, that we do not lack suitable women who will be able to carry out this responsibility. Amongst Indian women there are many who are socially conscious and who will be able to assume their responsibilities and steer the nation along the path of progress by addressing issues of poverty, ill health, illiteracy and discriminatory customs and laws.

You must have understood by now how you can intervene in governance by being an elected representative. However, there is another aspect of governance. This is the administrative side. Earlier people used to jest that after wearing the hat of learning, women will take to wearing shoes and socks and become judges and magistrates. Also that 'Podipishi' (Aunt Podi) will wear a gown and pronounce judgments in the High Court. Now such rhymes evoke laughter. According to the first section of the Fundamental Rights enacted by the new government, all citizens of India will enjoy equal opportunities and rights in every sphere. Hence there are now no obstacles to women becoming judges and magistrates. It has been clearly mentioned in Article 15 (b) that all citizens of India (women included), irrespective of caste or religion, will enjoy the same privileges in the workplace. Hence women will not be denied either government jobs or professional and vocational training. If equipped with appropriate education and skills, women can compete with men at any level, occupy the position deserved and earn a livelihood in government and private enterprises as magistrates, clerks, lawyers and barristers, doctors and engineers. Many contemporary women leaders have proved their competence and earned a good reputation as ministers, governors, in legislative assemblies and in the provincial governments. I believe that women will be able to preserve this reputation in a wider public sphere of work.

All said and done, there is one thing that demands attention and that concerns our social attitude. Despite all the power vested in women in the new Constitution, to be fully able to exercise that power there is an urgent need to bring about a change in the mindset of people. In other words, unless the prevalent discriminatory and oppressive social practices and legal disabilities are redressed, women will not be able to make full use of these rights. Primary among these are: 1) lack of opportunities and poor dissemination of girls' education which can only be redressed by making primary education compulsory; 2) underage marriages which result in both the mother and the child, who will be the future citizen of the nation, leading pitiful malnourished lives; 3) a daughter's right to inheritance in the paternal property whose absence has made this particular section of the Fundamental Rights quite meaningless.

Women need to realise today that this work could be done only by those men and women who are working towards the framing of progressive and reformative laws, through social awareness programmes, and by those who view the problems existing in society pragmatically. Women must become conscious that their problems can only be addressed by women, and, that whether it be in politics, administration or social work, it is only well-educated women who can join hands and take forward those mothers and sisters who have been left behind, and give a voice to what they want to say.

First published as 'Nari o Shasontantro'
('Women and Governance') in *Bharatbarsha*,
Jaistha 1360 BS (May-June 1954)

Translated by Sutanuka Ghosh

Can the Law Give Elderly Persons the Status they Deserve?

With persons over 65 years expected to be over 50 million by the year 2000 in India, the social services sector in our country will have to be geared up for the task of providing adequate services to this huge aged population if family support is not available to them. For gradually with the break-down of the old joint-family units particularly in the urban areas and with the growth of mobile nuclear families, more and more of the aged will have to take care of themselves.

That times are changing and traditional values and attitudes in the family and society are also changing in the matter of care for older persons and parents is very painful for us particularly for those of us who are of the older generation.

Recently the Haryana Government enacted a Bill that the responsibility of taking care of the elderly persons rests with their children. No dependent parents may remain neglected if they have adult and earning children.

Earlier, a mother could always claim maintenance from her children just as a wife could demand support from her husband. But in most cases 'mother' was taken care of in the family as a dependent member. Whether or not she lived in comfort enjoying a proper status in the family could not be ensured.

This brings me to a case we came across in 1975 (International Year of Women) in Calcutta where a retired IPS Officer was staying in his father's house with his family, his mother and an unmarried sister. He let out one flat in the three-storeyed house, had one for his own family, while his mother and sister lived on the ground floor. The mother had no pension or income, and nor did the sister. The rent collected from the flat was not shared by him with his mother and sister. They appealed to the Legal Aid Committee of the All India Women's Conference and wanted a part of the rent income which was refused by him. We tried our best to settle some reasonable amount for the dependent mother and sister. But he was so powerful and adamant that he refused and would not agree or listen to us or arrange for a family settlement.

Then we came across another case where a widowed mother shared her husband's house with her sons but as she had a widow's pension the eldest son set up a separate kitchen, did not support her, and told his younger brother, who was also a dependent in the same house, to fend for himself.

There is the sad case of a retired person who spent all his savings to educate his eldest son and to send him abroad, and had to starve with his wife and his other two children in Calcutta. The boy used to remit some amount but after he got married and went abroad again with his wife, he stopped sending any money for the family. The father would not write to him for a monthly remittance in spite of his wife asking him to do so, because he felt it was beneath his dignity to go to his son with a begging bowl.

There are random examples where an earning member does not or did not support his parents.

Will it be possible to ensure making law effective if the party is unwilling to help? Will the father or mother be willing to go to the court to assert his or her right?

A relationship which is based on love, respect and mutual understanding is put to test as it becomes an obligation on the part of the children, without the real bond of love. Rapid social change, particularly the changing nature of attitudes in family relationships, is ruining our sense of devotion to duty and respect for the elderly. Definitely there is a need for a law, but the enforcement will not be easy until the matter of obligations to one's elders as outlined in our traditional society is emphasised at an early age, so that children learn to share with others in a common household.

I feel one should try to establish a code of conduct in the community where young and old live together, share the joys and sorrows and also the duties of the household. As far as possible one-unit families should not be encouraged but rather a three-tier family in the same home, older people on the ground floor, and a son or daughter on the other floor or flat so that each can fall back on the other when there is need.

Society in the USA is taking such steps now where three units or four units stay in the same building but with separate establishments, just as we had in our old joint families in urban areas. You can see such joint families in and around old Calcutta even today.

For rural areas we must follow the East Bengal or Kerala pattern where in the same compound parents, brothers and sisters live in separate blocks or cottages each with their own establishment. This will enable them to leave young children in the care of the elderly. Working parents will be able to depend on the relatives who will share the care of children with affection and love, and not have to worry about leaving children in the hands of paid maids or in crèches which are seldom available in the rural areas.

So far we have talked about persons who can afford to maintain their parents but would not do so because of callousness and disregard for traditional values so to speak. But the other groups who are middle or lower class households can only help elders by keeping them with their family which may suffer from stress due to poverty, and may ill treat or exploit them by putting undue pressure to help with household work. In these cases, the 'Law' cannot help the elderly for obvious reasons.

Also, we must remember that the 'Law' is but an instrument, it cannot function on its own, until such time as someone appeals to the authorities for remedial measures. Therefore, a 'Caring Law' is important for those who can ask for a remedy, but it cannot change the attitude in the family if they have no regard for traditional values.

I would like to quote from Sri MS Gore.

> There is still time, while the vestiges of the traditional respect for the elderly in the family remain, for sensitising the community to these potential problems so that they can be minimised. A mere enlistment [*sic*] of the rights of the elderly in imitation of the rights of the child will not serve much purpose unless an awareness of the problems which are likely to arise is created and unless attitudes change and supplementary services are gradually brought into existence.

In the end, I would like to say that for this purpose new and innovative programmes both at the state and non-governmental sector will have to be developed to cater to this increasing human problem which cannot be washed away. Increasingly society will have to find the resources and sensitivity that are required to tackle the problem of the aged. One of the major thrust areas would be to utilise the experience and productive capacity of this population for whom interesting programmes can be drawn up.

Even with greater awareness of the problem of the aged, and even if the institutional and legal frameworks are put in place, it would still be extremely difficult for the problem to be tackled unless there is a much greater awareness amongst the community. The Government of India by fulfilling part 9 of its obligations under Article 41 [the Right to Public Assistance], by providing old age pensions and health insurance could provide some form of economic support. We in India over the centuries have built up many forms of traditional support for the elderly. We should not accept and follow western models which are not only costly but also lack in the levels of interaction that is necessary to keep the family units cohesive in a fast-changing social order. Our legislation should be framed keeping in mind past practices and our cultural heritage so that the elderly can be used as a huge resource base rather than be considered parasites on society.

Family Violence and Married Women

The problem of crimes against women is not new. Women in Indian society have been victims of humiliation, torture and exploitation for a long time. However, since the late 1960s and early 1970s three main types of family violence towards married women—dowry deaths, wife-battering and intra-familial murders—are being reported more. The issue of violence towards married women has been transformed from a private matter to a public problem. Although violence typically refers to physical aggression it can also be applied to psychological stress that causes suffering or trauma.

In our society, the majority of marriages are arranged by parents or by elders in the family. As a result, after marriage a young bride has to enter a new life amongst family members who are complete strangers, including her husband. It is the girl who is supposed to make all the adjustments and obey the wishes and commands of her husband and in-laws. After marriage the woman becomes the property of her husband. Even though society does not say that a husband has a right to beat his wife, it is assumed that he has a right to make her bow to his wishes. So when a man cannot tame his wife in any other way he uses force. Aggression and violence are considered to be male qualities and the man who is not assertive in marriage becomes an object of ridicule. Most women who suffer stress or strain or are victims of even violence do not want to say so

With Phulrenu Guha. In 1960 Ashoka Gupta was appointed a member of the Central Social Welfare Board, and Phulrenu Guha took her place as Chairman of the State Welfare Board

lest such disclosures hurt her dignity. A woman is supposed to bear her sufferings silently.

It is socially accepted that within the family the man is the 'master', the 'superior' and 'dominant' person and the woman is inferior. She has to be submissive. Women themselves accept the subordinate role within marriage unquestioningly.

In cases of women being ill-treated within the family, persecuted or beaten by their husbands or in-laws, no one is usually prepared to help them—neither their parents, nor relatives, nor the police. People are hesitant to interfere in family matters which are regarded as private. These helpless battered women have nowhere to go. That is why it is so essential for the women's movement to take up this issue of violence in the family both physical and mental. It is necessary to find out *why* violence occurs, *what* forms it takes and *what* can we do to stop it.

Several studies undertaken by women's groups and social workers reveal that causes of violence are:

(a) arguments over money i.e. financial problems
(b) jealousy and suspicion of the woman's character
(c) instigation by in-laws and ill-treatment by in-laws

(d) housework—the wife is accused of being inefficient or incompetent, lazy and lethargic
(e) alcohol consumption by husband
(f) woman's desire to work outside the home, or woman's self-esteem ('she thinks too much of herself')
(g) disputes about children
(h) extra-marital affairs on the part of the husband or the wife
(i) husband's cruel nature, or husband's having experienced violent and abusive childhood
(j) nagging and irritable behaviour of wives
(k) too much interference by wives in their husbands' affairs

Dowry of course is an important factor behind violence. The genesis of dowry deaths lies in the tension created by persistent demands, accompanied by torture. The greed for money and consumer goods encourages family members to take the bride's life. Violence takes many forms, such as beating with hands, blows, beating with sticks or iron rods, beating with utensils or knives and ladles, excessive sexual demands and perversions, burning women, etc. The injuries suffered include deep cuts requiring stitches, broken bones, nervous breakdowns.

There are some myths about violence against married women which need to be destroyed. The first is that such violence is perpetrated only in poor families and that middle-class women do not get beaten. Women from all sections of society, belonging to different religions and all socio-economic classes are victims of violence, though violence is more prevalent in lower-class households because of economic stress, unemployment and economic deprivation. The man who commits violence is always from the lower class, frustrated in his job, alcoholic, a paranoid, aggressive in his relations with the world at large.

Despite being humiliated and physically and mentally tortured women stay on with their husbands partly because of their childhood conditioning to see marriage as the ultimate goal for a woman and to think breaking a marriage will bring humiliation to her parental family. If she has younger sisters they may not get married. But even some

In Orissa

of those who would like to walk out of the marriage cannot do so because of (1) lack of education; (2) economic dependence; (3) lack of support-structures; (4) difficulty in obtaining divorce/job/house; (5) burden of child care. As a result these women become passive, resigned and negative in their approach.

Apart from wife-battering, married women are also sometimes murdered by family members. These murders are inspired by factors such as illicit relations, feelings of revenge, the desire to remarry to get another dowry, or to get rid of a person who is to get a share in the property, etc. Many murders are disguised as suicides or even accidents. In many cases the victim's kin not only fail to get protection from the police but cannot even turn to the law courts for redress.

Suggested remedies: Our ideas and understanding about the causes of family violence towards married women will influence the steps we take to prevent it. First of all, we must try to change our notion that the family is a hierarchical institution in which the man is the head and therefore superior. Husband and wife are equal partners and must share all work and responsibilities.

1. A step towards this is if we stop having arranged marriages and allow boys and girls to choose their own partners.
2. Another factor which contributes to wife-battering is the total economic dependence of the woman on the man. Lack of education and job skills make it difficult for many middle-class women to leave their husbands. Women must, therefore, be given education and provided with employment-oriented courses.
3. There must be more homes for women who want shelter when their lives are threatened—short-stay homes.
4. The women who decide to break away need free legal aid.
5. Hostels for women with children.
6. We need to create a new awareness in society so that the attitude of doctors, counsellors, institutions, social workers and the police is more sympathetic towards victims of marital violence.
7. Sex-education for women and men.
8. Marriage counselling centres.
9. Forming Mahila Atma-Raksha Samitis in every mohalla to fight this aspect of women's oppression.
10. Women police officers should be available to speak to any woman who comes to the police station for help.
11. Police should have the power to take preventive action.
12. Government should introduce legislation on the same lines as the Domestic Violence Act in England to protect married women within the family.*

Published in ROSHNI,
Journal of the All India Women's Conference,
July-September 2004

* The Protection of Women from Domestic Violence Act was passed by the Indian Parliament in 2005.

Unveiling of the portrait of Bhikaiji Cama in the Central Hall of Parliament, August 3, 1989. Also in picture, Vice-President Dr Shankar Dayal Sharma and Prime Minister Rajiv Gandhi

In 1999 Ashoka Gupta looked back at her long association with the AIWC

Reminiscences of a Former President

I still wonder how the All India Women's Conference reached the remotest parts of India and touched the hearts of women within the four walls of homes so widely separated from each other, located in far-flung areas, from Rajasthan to the pilgrim town of Puri, Orissa. I recall the letters of Anindita Devi (mother of the late Amiya Chakraborty), a progressive thinker, written from her sickbed in Puri (under her pseudonym 'Banganari'[35]) to my mother Jyotirmoyee Debi, a young widow living in purdah in the princely state of Jaipur. They were trying to get a glimpse of the world through the window of the AIWC, exchanging views on how the AIWC should act/react to the proposals related to Hindu marriage, the Sarda Act, the Age of Consent and the Hindu Code Bill. They condemned, discussed and also supported many moves and resolutions passed by the AIWC in the annual and half-yearly sessions in the second decade of this century.

Perhaps I became inquisitive and absorbed ideas of women's position in society through their writings, letters and articles. I am sure our generation started thinking along with the pioneers about the role of women and their status in society from that time.

I became a member of the AIWC in 1936 in Calcutta at the time of the Hindu Code Bill hearings where my mother used to give evidence. I continued to take active part in fund-raising campaigns

[35] Translates as Bengali Woman.

At a meeting

as a member of the AIWC in the Dacca Branch. I helped set up a welfare organisation in Jessore and coordinated the activities of voluntary organisations which had been relocated to Krishnanagar during the war after the bombing of Calcutta in 1942, and I helped set up an AIWC branch in Nadia. It was a new experience to work with personalities like Lady Abala Bose, Kumudini Bose and Charulata Mukherjee of AIWC Calcutta Branch.

Relief work at Bankura during the famine of 1943 and our efforts for the welfare of the distressed under the leadership of Usha Haldar brought energy and new life into the organisation of the AIWC at Bankura. I was entrusted with setting up one of the Homes of the Save the Children Committee at Bankura under the auspices of the AIWC led by Vijaya Lakshmi Pandit, President of AIWC in 1943-44, and helped again in economic programmes under the guidance of Kamaladevi Chattopadhyaya, President of AIWC in 1944-45. I attended the AIWC meetings in Delhi and Bombay in 1943 and 1944. During the riots in Noakhali in 1946, under the leadership and guidance of Nellie Sengupta (then President of the AIWC, Chittagong

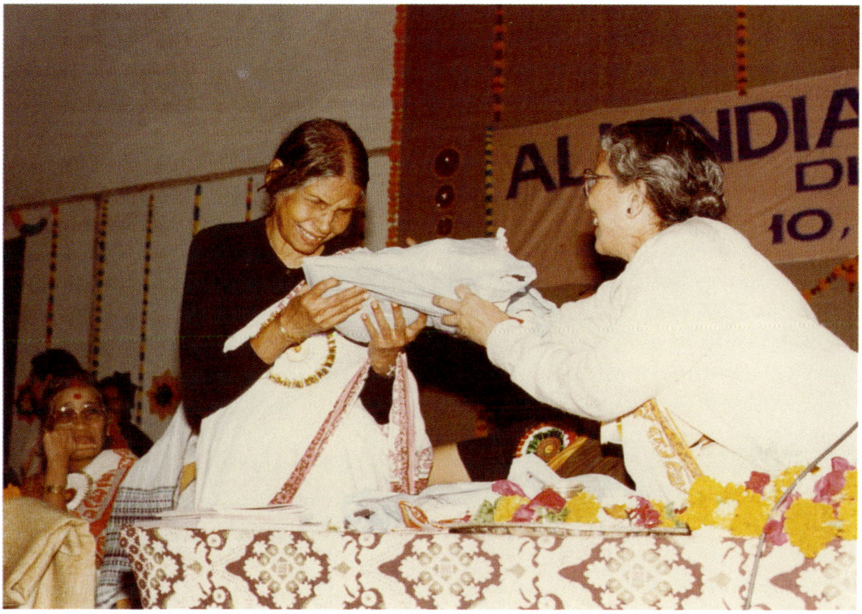

With Lakshmi Menon (AIWC President 1955-58)

Branch), I volunteered to act as a leader of the Volunteers on behalf of the Branch and gave up the security of home life and devoted myself exclusively to bring relief to the uprooted humanity, and comfort to the panic-stricken multitude, while at the same time trying to restore communal harmony by an appeal to the better sense of the majority community under the inspiring guidance of Gandhiji. My trek to and my stay with my small daughter in the remote Harijan villages of Noakhali to give succour to affected people under the direction of Thakkar Bapa and as advised by Gandhiji is something that I consider one of my life's most cherished experiences.

I was a member of the Standing Committee of the AIWC Central Body from 1943 till today. I was able to organise the Youth Wing of AIWC as Member-in-charge in 1970-74. As President of AIWC, I had tried to lead the Branches to work as well-knit units in their own areas and, as Head of the Department of the Constitution of AIWC, I had helped to set up Branches in new areas and to set them right where they did not fall in line with the policy, aims and rules and regulations of AIWC.

With Margaret Alva, Union Minister of State, Women and Children, 1989

I have learned a lot during my Presidentship. In five years' time, I also had the experience of evaluating the socio-economic programme of the Central Social Welfare Board, touring several states of India with the experts in our Committee (a copy of our report is in the AIWC Library). My experience as Chairman of the Board and subsequently as a member of the Central Social Welfare Board for ten years helped me make the evaluation practical from the point of view of the NGOs who begin such projects.

Then the problem of ageing started surfacing, along with the issue of battered and tortured women. We set up our Old Age Home in Brindavan for the older Vaishnav pilgrims who, at the end of their life, wanted to die at the feet of Radha Rani in Brindavan's temple town. This was followed by the setting up of our infirmary. Both are running well. I understand the Short Stay Homes in six places of India have been very successful in relieving distress and it was an eye-opener to see what sort of cruelty is inflicted within the four walls of the home on our helpless women.

Inaugural procession, Golden Jubilee of the AIWC, Pune, 1987

All these are about my association with the AIWC in my younger days and as President. But a great change has taken place since then. We, the women, have been silent spectators to the brutal events that are taking place all over the country over the past decades—whether these are due to family disputes, religious fundamentalism, economic disparities or ethnic conflict is a matter for research. In the changing socio-cultural and economic context it is natural that the institutional framework and values are bound to change, but that does not mean that society will go back to the practices of earlier times. Social and religious institutions have identified women primarily as carriers of traditions, and a public culture dominated by men has perpetuated an 'approved image' of women, created through a selective use of religious/cultural idioms. If the status of women is to change, it is imperative that this social exploitation be checked.

Three-quarters of a century is a fairly long period in the life of any organisation and the AIWC which started in 1926 can look back with some satisfaction at what it is has done so far. But it would be wrong to

With Pratibha Patil, member, Rajya Sabha, 1987

rest on our oars and think that we have reached our goal. I personally feel that each one of us should take up this challenge. We must establish closer links with our far-flung branches in remote areas. I feel with the new leadership we shall be able to widen our horizons and extend our activities to areas which will promote communal harmony and national integration, and develop the tolerance to understand each other's point of view both in the family as well as in the community. I feel that we have not done this to the extent needed.

The AIWC also should play a major role in bringing about a social revolution by changing the behavioural patterns in our society. We have also to see that our social thinking, too, comes in line with the aspirations of our rural community for technological advancement.

I feel if a cadre of women workers can be created to go round and study domestic problems at the doorstep, millions of voiceless women may be benefitted. I admit that this is somewhat ambitious but a start may be made in some selected areas where circumstances are favourable. We may also utilise government resources to undertake this work and render whatever help they need from us.

Above: Condolence meeting for Vijaya Lakshmi Pandit (AIWC President, 1943), December 1990; Below: With Kamaladevi Chattopadhyaya, 1988

This will help us to reach the ageing who are neglected in their homes and religious places due to the craze for single-unit families and the break-up of joint families, and also the abandoned women and girls who need shelter and training to establish them in life. The programmes of the AIWC have expanded manifold. It is not a matter of how many short-stay homes for the aged or crèches we run but in what measure we have contributed in the decision-making process,

At a workshop

both in non-government organisations and at the government level through panchayats, state legislative assemblies, and Parliament.

I strongly feel that AIWC's role as a campaigner should not be forgotten. Momentous changes are taking place. The thrust today is towards forward-looking strategies for 2000 AD. AIWC played a historic role in the field of education, particularly education for girls, in

With members of a Russian delegation, 1990

promoting health and planned parenthood by establishing pioneering institutions, working on social legislation affecting women and labour, initiating welfare services for children, and above all securing political rights for women. We would be failing in our duty as campaigners if we slackened our concerted effort in these directions in building a women's movement.

When we take up such an ambitious programme of campaigning all over the country through our AIWC branches, should we not allocate resources and plan a budget clearly defining our priority so that the Branches can utilise those funds to successfully carry out those projects through Branches in remote areas. For this we must continuously train young women as campaigners and leaders of project management for the welfare of women and children, economic development of women in rural areas, for family planning, for education, adult literacy, utilisation of energy and scientific technology with the clear aim of changing the attitude of men and the political leaders.

If the AIWC were to take advantage of those resources by preparing projects for the Branches, that grassroots-level workers can devote time for survey work and personal contacts with women of all communities, while a strong central secretariat can prepare projects and set apart funds for development, and define priorities in addition to utilising funds from the Ministry.

We should try to guide the Branches through seminars and training schemes in regional centres instead of at the headquarters. Funds have to be set apart also for special programmes like the eradication of illiteracy.

To have a real women's movement in the country it is imperative that various organisations should work unitedly. If all welfare organisations can work together, our combined endeavour would avoid duplication of efforts and would help to run a successful and smooth campaign. The All-India Committee for Eradication of Illiteracy is one such example where seven national organisations have joined hands, and resources are being pooled. In the move to achieve a fair deal for women, the joint effort by over ten all-India organisations led to the Act on National Commission on Women being revised and several amendments incorporated including 33% membership in panchayats. The Human Rights Commission has also been trying to do justice to women's causes.

The AIWC is concerned with the cause of women as a whole, but as a purely non-political body we should urge the Government to give justice to women irrespective of the faith they follow and should treat them as being under a common civil code as defined in our constitution. AIWC has always held that a Common Civil Code would strengthen the country's unity and integrity. Women will have a fair deal as citizens of this country. Public opinion has to be moulded to make social reforms acceptable to the people. An important part of the Directive Principles of State Policy of the Constitution is Article 44, which enjoins the state to work towards a uniform civil code for all citizens. We have to educate public opinion so that the resistance to social reforms founded on sentiments and fears is removed. In my opinion, parliament should enact Muslim, Christian and Parsi Family Codes on the lines of the Hindu Code as a prelude to a common civil code. As an alternative an optional law on the lines of the Special Marriage Act, with an obligatory chapter on human rights, should be enacted.

I would like to repeat what I stated in 1986 when I took over as President—that we must remain non-political, which means staying away from party politics. Our aim should be to generate an atmosphere where the missionary takes precedence over the mercenary. A new spirit of selflessness should be our goal. This is not to suggest that political power is not important but that alone cannot be the ultimate aim. Political participation is only the means to an end. In fact effective political participation by women, and acquisition of a decision-making authority in the nation's body politic should be only a part of our programme. Our battle must be waged on all five fronts—political, social, economic, religious and ideological. We must strive for greater economic participation by women, fight for freedom from age-old social as well as religious constraints on women, and challenge the traditional cult of domesticity and the implied inferiority of women. The road is long and the hurdles high, but at the end the rewards will be rich.

USSR, 1958

Travels

Clockwise from right: Brazil 1962; West Germany 1969; USSR, Leningrad 1958

Clockwise from right: Sweden, 1990; Russia; West Berlin 1969; Tour of the USA, 1956, newspaper report

With Mahasweta Devi, writer and fellow-activist

Friends

Top to bottom: With daughter Shakuntala, at a meeting of the Bharat Scouts and Guides, 2002; With Tara Bhattacharya, Gandhiji's granddaughter, and Yasmeen Sengupta, Kasturba Gandhi Memorial Trust meeting, 2000; With Dr Vina Mazumdar, 2003, at the launch of The Trauma and the Triumph

Top to bottom: With Dr Maitreyi Bose at the Crafts Bazaar, Kolkata Maidan, 1989. The theme that year was 'Women's Empowerment'; With sister Anjali Chatterji and Saroj Sood, at a meeting of the Indian Society for Sponsorship and Adoption, 2007; With Gopal Gandhi, Gandhiji's grandson, then Governor of West Bengal, at a Mahila Samity function at Rajpur, 2005. In 1947 the Governor Shri Rajagopalachari (Gopal's other grandfather) had given space in the Raj Bhavan for the West Bengal Emergency Relief Committee. This became the Mahila Seva Samity, of which Ashoka Gupta was a founder-member

Ashoka Gupta, 2002

Her years living with extended families, and her long years of involvement with the AIWC, the Mahila Samity, and the Scouts and Guides, meant that Ashoka had a wide range of friends extending across India and abroad, and across generations. In the following essays she recalls some of them...

Remembering Sisters-in-arms

Sneharani Kanjilal

Whenever I think of Sneha I remember a tranquil, calm and smiling face, a bright vermilion mark on the forehead, a colourful saree with the *anchal* drawn partly across her head. There was a request for a song at the Duttapara Camp in Noakhali and with the harmonium before her she started singing in her easy melodious voice: 'I bow before you, O fearless One'. The instinctive expression of respect, faith and passion in the song made one feel as if we had all joined together in a prayer.

Sneha was pleasant and sweet. It seemed as if she was very soft and gentle and would get easily tired. Sneha and I spent eight long months with her son and my daughter in the same village, in the same room and often on the same bed in Noakhali's riot-torn Tumchar. I have never witnessed Sneha display tiredness or impatience amidst strenuous labour, long treks, complicated situations or debates with malicious people, or discussion sessions with the villagers that stretched till midnight after an entire day spent in relief distribution. It was characteristic of Sneha to ease tense situations with her radiant smile. There was no one as adept as Sneha at lightening the atmosphere with a jest or a few words spoken in the Noakhali dialect, thus bringing to a halt the tense disputation. After visiting Sucheta Kripalani's camp in Duttapara I learnt that Sneha had decided to accompany me to Tumchar. At that time, I had no hesitation in saying, and I said this to Sneha many times, that I feared that Sneha would not be able to withstand the hard conditions. When I further learned that Sneha was the daughter-in-law of a well-to-do family, a householder running a large family consisting of her ten sons and four daughters, household staff and relations, I was apprehensive that with such close ties of affection in the remote hamlet of Tumchar, Sneha would not be able to keep at bay the demands of her family. However, neither her husband Monomohan Kanjilal nor her sons and daughters hindered her work. Apart from her two youngest sons and sometimes Monomohanbabu, none of her other children visited her while we lived in this village; nor did she express any distress at not having seen them for long. Later when I saw her at home amidst the diurnal household chores, I saw how effortlessly she had slipped back into the role of the householder. It seemed as if there was a change of role with change of place. Yet, even while performing hard ceaseless labour for her family, Sneha regularly accompanied her husband to numerous political programmes and discussions.

Just as Gandhiji's call beckoned us all, it drew Sneha out of the bounds of her home. She suddenly arrived in Chaumohani on November 7, 1946, leaving behind her happy family life with her husband and children. From there on to Duttapara, and then to Gandhiji's camp in Srirampur. Holding on to Gandhiji's inspiration and instruction she arrived together with the workers at Duttapara. I was first introduced to Sneha at Duttapara. At that time Gandhiji had asked us to work in Harijan villages. Thakkar Bapa was in Charruhita and more workers were needed there. I got Sneha as my companion when I elected to go to the western part of that region to Tumchar.

The exchange of thoughts and ideas that takes place when we work with the same ideals, the same goals and the same beliefs, and the affection and friendship that this fosters, established the bond between Sneha and me. We never thought we were working separately. Whether it was relief, rehabilitation or meetings, none of my tasks in this region would be complete without Sneha's participation. Also as Noakhali's daughter-in-law she had an advantage. She easily acquired a familiarity with the local dialect and mode of pronunciation and that facilitated her interaction with the village men and women. At Haimchor, on February 28, 1947, Gandhiji gave us our final work instructions. Sneha, Sucheta Kripalani, I and some 8 to 10 fellow-workers were instructed to continue working in all the camps. Sneha followed every word of the instruction. Many workers returned home after Gandhiji left. However, none of those working in the villages in the Harijan areas left because they felt unable to leave their ever-smiling and affectionate elder sister Sneha and go elsewhere.

Everyone who visited the camp in those days would remember how Sneha used to keep herself immersed in the work through the day, every day. Without Sneha it was impossible to conduct the work marches in the mornings, the rehabilitation programmes in the afternoons and the prayer meetings in the evenings. Sneha's musical training and melodious voice enlivened the prayer meetings. Her warm affection drew every woman and child of the village to her. If I was ever irritated when someone repeatedly asked for a saree or some other help, Sneha with her characteristic smile would say, 'Ashokadi, permission withheld for a single saree!' Hearing Sneha one could not help but laugh.

This was our Sneha—everyone's Snehadi who served destitute women in remote villages, and Sneharani Kanjilal, wife and favourite aide to Noakhali's well-known lawyer Monomohan Kanjilal. She was radiant and fulfilled, with her husband and children, good fortune and pecuniary wealth. From this aspect she was someone to be envied. On the other hand, I do not remember ever having seen someone like Sneha cope with a sudden reversal in fortune in the way she did, cloaking her tears in her smile and with great patience, will-power and unflinching commitment, holding fast to the reins of her household after her husband passed away.

In the various spheres of life Sneha demonstrated a temperament to battle obstacles and adversities. The resoluteness of her character has enhanced her image before the people; she is esteemed and loved by all. She was ever eager to serve others but never sought anything for herself. Whether it be the All India Women's Conference or emergency relief work, the Sanjukta Mahila Parishad (Joint Women's Committee) or rehabilitation of refugees, it was almost impossible for any women's organisation to function without Sneha's participation. (Much later) Renuka Ray invited the same Sneha to Bongaon to work in the Bangladesh refugee camp. At this time Sneha's health had broken down and the radiance had been considerably dimmed but she remained simple and large-hearted. I have witnessed Sneha's dedicated, focussed, untiring work day after day, refusing to heed caution. Perhaps, through her passionate work Sneha was able to turn back the clock and relive the days of her youth.

She was dear to us and was admired by many more. This simple, artless, non-egotistical person was absolutely unassuming, just like her firm, spare and clear handwriting. She may not have had formal and functional learning, yet she was able to get the better of many through her discerning, sensitive and unpretentious manner. Those of us who have seen and known Sneha closely will want to hold on to her through some beautiful memories. Today, having gathered all our love and admiration, she is waiting somewhere where we cannot reach her despite our numerous fervent pleas, where she is still and contemplative like a photo stuck in a frame. Like scattered photographs, Sneha has left behind in our bereft lives some reserves of priceless memories—her affable way of speaking, her love and deep compassion, a soft and beautiful face, and a tranquil and tender grace that lent her an unparalleled luminosity.

This was appended to *Noakhalir Durjoger Din*

Translated by Sutanuka Ghosh

Sucheta Kripalani (1908–1974)

Of the girl children that were born in riot-ravaged Noakhali, about eighty per cent were named Sucheta or Kripalani by their parents. I had laughed and said, 'Kripalani is a last name, how can it become a first name?' The villagers replied, 'She had taken pity on us, *kripa*, and that gave us courage and strength. In those traumatic days, who else was there who stood by us like a mother and listened to our sorrow with love, compassion and feelings. In naming our baby daughters after her we want to keep alive this memory.'

When trying to fathom the respect with which these words are laden, one remembers, 'Amongst humankind glorious is he, who lives on in people's memory'. Sucheta Kripalani was such a person whom we cannot forget, whom it is not possible to forget.

One can come close to people if one has firmness of character, is honest, and loves the nation and the people. Sucheta Kripalani had that ability. She also had the ability to transform vision into reality, to lead and to put to use all constructive workers irrespective of their political allegiance. No one could say 'no' to her. She had a comprehensive knowledge of the legal machinery. Sucheta did not defer to anyone. Whatever needed to be done, she was able to get it done by top (British) officials.

Once we received news that in a Noakhali village an abducted girl was living with a local family as their daughter-in-law. The District Magistrate was arriving to investigate. Sucheta Kripalani was asked to be there at that time. The District Magistrate was an Irish officer, Mr McInerny, ICS. When he arrived with a police force, Sucheta was there. The master of the family said, it is true the girl is here with us. However, she is an adult and has married my son voluntarily. This is not a case of abduction. They married because they were in love. Mr McInerny was fluent in Bengali and he summoned the girl and spoke to her. The girl looked a wreck, quite weak. By merely nodding her head she indicated that she had come willingly and would stay there.

Sucheta requested the Magistrate, 'Please take her to a separate room and enquire. That will reveal the real state of affairs.' The Magistrate replied, 'This is a love marriage, what else is there to enquire?' Sucheta flashed fire. She asked, 'Please Mr McInerny, please give me one concrete case of a love affair between the communities after the riots from October 10 to this day. This is not a case of love marriage. Take evidence in a separate room so that the girl can speak the truth.' Due to her insistence the girl was taken to a separate room, just the Magistrate and the girl. Everyone else remained outside. When the girl looked everywhere and saw that no one else was there, weeping piteously she fell at the sahib's feet. 'Please take me away from here immediately. I seek your refuge.'

The sahib understood everything. Yet he sent for Sucheta Kripalani and said, 'Where will I take her now? Let's wait a while and see.' Sucheta replied, 'With the powers that you have you could keep her in any ashram or even in a jail. But if you do that the news will spread in the whole district. Even the whole of India will know that you failed to rescue an abducted girl and give her shelter. The more you delay the more intense will be the agitation. You will not be able to maintain law and order. Please transfer her from this district to another with police escort. The girl is an adult. Hence if she refuses to accept this love marriage, what right do you have to keep her here any further?' Her words had the right effect. The girl was taken under police custody and after spending two nights at Jogendrakumar Majumdar's residence in Chaumohoni, she was sent to the women's institute at Comilla's Kasturba Gandhi National Memorial Trust. She received medical treatment here and after her recovery, an idealistic young man married her. I heard the marriage was happy.

Sucheta's forceful personality, her scholarship, prison terms spent with the freedom fighters, participation in civil disobedience made her an extraordinary character. She made appropriate use of her valuable experiences in every aspect of life, whether it was the work at Noakhali or going underground to help the nationalists in the Quit India movement or, on Gandhiji's instruction, after the demise of Kasturba, establishing Kasturba Gandhi Memorial Trust branches and training centres for village workers in every state. She could venture unhesitatingly in all these spheres and work in a meticulously organised fashion.

Sucheta was born in 1908 in a Bengali family settled outside Bengal. Her father was Dr Surendranath Majumdar and her mother Premlata

Devi. All Brahmo teachings like freedom for women, clarity in thinking, were her heritage from her parents. She was a young lecturer at the Benares Hindu University when she met Acharya Kripalani. She married him in 1936, and resigned from teaching in 1939. Her career as a Congress worker began at this point. She did not look back after this and immersed herself completely in serving the community and nation. She also made significant contributions to the framing of the Constitution. Even in the Civil Disobedience movement, she played a leading role within the Congress. Having been born and brought up in Punjab, she was closely acquainted with freedom fighters and in the struggles throughout the country.

I met her during the Quit India Movement when she was in hiding in Bombay. After a session of the All India Women's Conference, I had to stay one night at Mridula Sarabhai's residence. At the dinner table, I saw that various women leaders who had gone underground, like Sucheta Kripalani and Aruna Asaf Ali, were quite happily living in Mridula Sarabhai's house. The police did not have any information. We met next at Noakhali. In the October of 1946 she came to the house of the Chittagong Commissioner, Carter. She had come with Acharya Kripalani, then Congress secretary, to discuss rescue and rehabilitation work in the riot-ravaged areas. Whether police protection would be available in the affected areas and how rescue operations would be done were discussed. It was decided that we, from the Chittagong women's group, would take part in this work. From this time onwards till the end of her life we remained close friends.

In April, when a cholera epidemic surfaced in the riot-affected areas, all instructions pertaining to the organisation of the medical teams' movements used to be issued from Duttapara by Sucheta and Dr Nripen Basu. When the epidemic struck the village next to my camp, I went in the morning to get the medical team. Dr Basu said, 'Didi, not today, we will send the team tomorrow or day after. Please stay here, rest and have some food.' I had left behind in the village my little daughter in the hope that I would be able to return with doctors. I turned pale. Sucheta said, 'You leave just now, you've left your daughter behind. I will myself ensure that the doctors and medicines reach there tomorrow morning.' She kept her word,

Remembering days gone by

and having perceived the state of my mind she made arrangements for a car to take me till Lakshmipur. Such was her ability quickly to take decisions on the spot.

Another time, at the end of May, orders arrived for my husband's transfer to the Partition Committee. I was alone with my children in the huge house at Chittagong. Sucheta was in Delhi at that time, in Gandhiji's camp. There was a lot of disturbance in Punjab. I sent a telegram asking her to come so that the work in the camps did not come to a stop. She arrived within four-five days and released me after gathering all the workers together and putting in place a proper system of organisation for all the camps.

Gandhiji had told her, 'Don't go now, Ashoka will manage everything.' Sucheta had replied, 'Bapu, Ashoka would never have called me unless it was very urgent.' She was one person who could easily tell Gandhiji—'Bapu, those who have hunger in their bellies, nothing to cover their nakedness, no roof over their heads, how will they sit down to pray for a change of heart and communal harmony? We must meet their fundamental material needs before we can expect them to listen to the message of peace and harmony.'

Sucheta loved her husband. After her release from prison in 1945 she had thought that she would rest and spend some time with him. Sucheta herself told me this. However, when she went to meet Gandhiji, he said, 'I was thinking about you. I have some urgent work at hand—the Kasturba Trust has been established in memory of Ba. You take charge of this as the organising secretary and establish branches in every state so that this women-run organisation provides care to rural women and trains them to become self-reliant.'

Then we had our bloodied Independence. Caring little for her own life, Sucheta started working for the Punjab refugees in the townships, work centres and relief camps, doing rehabilitation work in the colonies. At that point the refugee influx from East Bengal had not yet started. Had she had the time to work for them then perhaps the refugees in West Bengal would not have suffered.

Over time she became a member of Parliament, Labour Minister of Uttar Pradesh, and then India's first woman Chief Minister. I do not think I have ever seen such a dedicated worker and someone who loved her motherland so much.

Gandhiji had said about her, 'Sucheta is such a person whose valiant courage and rare character has enhanced the status of Indian women.'

That is so very true.

This was appended to *Noakhalir Durjoger Din*

Translated by Sutanuka Ghosh

Lakshmi Menon (1897–1994)

It seems as if she has not left us. Perhaps I will open my letterbox and find a neatly written inland letter from Lakshmi giving either her views on the current situation of the Kasturba Gandhi National Memorial Trust or the future of the All-India Committee for Eradication of Illiteracy amongst Women or a simple greeting letter for the Bengali New Year or Bijoya Dashami.

She was very particular in this respect I think because, she had an early teaching assignment here in Calcutta in the Gokhale Memorial School & College, where the occasions of the Bengali New Year in mid-April and Dassehra in September or October were meticulously celebrated. Even now, anyone residing in Bengal cannot get away from the festive spirit of Naba Barsha or Bijoya Dashami, whatever may be his or her caste, community or state. One of her last letters, which I received just a few weeks before her death, wishing me a happy Bijoya Dashami and complaining that I had not wished her (quoted below) read—'This is Puja time in Calcutta, and everyone sends Bijoya greetings to friends and relatives. I want to send you greetings for this day and wish all the best to you and your family, Lakshmi'.

We had known each other since 1944 when I attended the half-yearly conference in Bombay. There was a galaxy of social workers adorning the dais—Sarojini Naidu, Vijaya Lakshmi Pandit, Kamaladevi Chattopadhyay, Rameshwari Nehru, Rani Rajwade and many others whose names I did not know. It was like a 'Rajsabha'. One could not miss in that group a young and vocal person who was none other than Lakshmi Menon. One could not but admire her for her pleasant manners and extraordinarily sharp rejoinders when various issues came up for discussion. There were two more of her age group whom we also liked—Purnima Banerjee and Lilamani Naidu. We were newcomers, and awestruck with their command over English and knowledge about the condition of women in the country, be it in the coalmines, tea gardens or in the jute factories. For those of us who were new to this forum, it was not only instructive but an eye-opener, as this opened up the horizon of women's sphere of activities beyond the four walls of the home. She encouraged us to speak in the conference on resolutions which were written by the Drafting

Committee where Lakshmi Menon, Renuka Ray, Purnima and Lilamani were indispensable.

In 1946, Harsha Mehta and Lakshmi took the lead in drafting the AIWC pamphlet on women's rights and duties and her status in society.

Some years later when she was President of the AIWC, I suddenly received a very warm letter asking me to join a delegation to the USSR on an invitation from the Soviet Women's Committee. It was such a pleasant surprise to be included in a team consisting of Mrs Mitha Lam, who was the leader, Mrs Masuma Begum, Smt Tapati Mukherjee, Smt Vishalakshmi Narayanaswami, and Smt Nirmala Desai. It was a study tour of one month, and we were to travel from north to south USSR, the Central Asian region and the Black Sea Coast. Laughingly, she said that when the Soviet Women's delegation visited us in India we should be able to host them. We readily agreed and left for the USSR for a month in 1958. Lakshmi always gave opportunities to new workers to gain experience and would gave them guidance. Years later, in 1971, she caught me at Bombay Airport, and asked me and Tara Sathe to serve as Trustees of the Kasturba Gandhi National Memorial Trust (KGNMT). Since then, we worked in the rural areas where KGNMT had its centres and also in the branches of AIWC which she had set up and developed. She took great pains to visit the rural centres and meet the workers. She was very affectionate and was very much loved by her colleagues in Calcutta, Patna, Lucknow, Delhi and Bombay, so that, all over India, wherever she went, she had a home to welcome her, and AIWC/KGNMT colleagues and workers who looked forward to her visit.

Her last dream was to make all women of India literate by 2000 AD. The All-India Committee for Eradication of Illiteracy amongst Women in India was set up twelve years back to create a band of workers who would make this a campaign and a successful project. I read a paper at the UN-NGO Forum on this project, which was drawn up by Smt Lakshmi Menon involving several major women's organisations in India—KGNMT, All India Women's Conference, National Council of Women in India, Women's Christian Association, Bharatiya Gramin Mahila Sangha, Women's Studies Centres, and later on others, who set up state committees to implement this challenging programme.

The international NGO community at this Forum highly appreciated this effort.

Before I conclude, I would like to quote from her letter to show how careful she was in planning a conference and giving guidance to juniors who may have had different views on issues settled at the national level.

On 28/1/94, she wrote to me:

> My dear Ashoka,
>
> A thousand apologies for the belated New Year's greetings to you...
>
> I will not be honest if I do not tell you how very concerned I am about your differences with...
>
> Whatever it is let us forget it and start afresh...Now it is time to do that. If you have any differences about the sphere of work it can be rectified. Please do that now.
>
> We are very short of workers and we are not people out for power but we want a band of dedicated workers pursuing ideals which emphasise service and sacrifice.
>
> I hope everything will go off wonderfully and harmoniously. We have many more challenges to meet and we should not quarrel, but live in harmony and smiles.
>
> Hope this finds you well and happy. May 1994 bring you happiness and fulfillment.
>
> Much love,
> Yours affectionately,
> Lakshmi Menon

I hope that in my reply and in my action I was able to convince her that I would try to live up to her ideals and expectations.

Usha Haldar

Renowned social worker, leader of the Brahmo Samaj and eminent doctor the late Prankrishna Acharya was her father. No doubt Smt Usha Haldar derived her courage, integrity and dedication to serve the community from him. She was born in an era when patriotism, integrity of character and service to others figured naturally in one's life. With her death in December 1981, not only did we lose our beloved sister and leader but it ended an era of selfless service. Some aspects of her work are narrated below.

The Bankura Maternity and Child Welfare Clinic were established by Usha Haldar in 1940. It was a full-fledged centre with a resident Health Visitor and a trained nurse. Not many people now remember that the foundation stone of this building was laid by Rabindranath Tagore. I recall how dearly Ushadi loved this place and how thorough she was in looking after all the administrative details of the organisation. The six surrounding villages were served by this Clinic and all the villagers knew 'Haldar Ma' and came to her for help, guidance and a word of encouragement.

When, in 1943, the Bengal famine was taking its toll in Bankura, Usha Haldar was able to draw all the workers of the All India Women's Conference out of their homes, and drew up a roster by which all members fanned out beyond the town towards the villages from where emaciated and starving families were trekking towards Bankura town with dying and hungry children in their arms. Some dropped these at the Sammilani Hospital gate. Those who could, walked up to Usha Haldar's Clinic. At the doorstep of the Clinic under Usha Haldar's guidance the members of the All India Women's Conference picked up the abandoned children, sometimes along with their mothers who were too weak to move, and gave them food and shelter at her clinic. A *shamiana* was put up, then several tents to accommodate all who needed shelter and food. Ushadi took the lead in collecting rations, milk and medicines, and procured the services of doctors, nurses and volunteers to help and revive the mothers and children who were on the verge of death.

Her leadership and quality of heart was such that workers took up difficult responsibilities without a murmur as if inspired by her,

Recalling other people, other places

sometimes even neglecting their other commitments. It was a joy to work with her because she did not spare herself and remained on her feet from early in the morning till very late at night. Without her guidance it would not have been possible to set up a unit of Save the Children Home at Bankura which was inaugurated by Smt Vijaya Lakshmi Pandit, the then President of the All India Women's Conference, who paid a visit to that famine-stricken area in 1943 and urged AIWC members to work with her to save hundreds of children who were facing starvation and death.

Usha Haldar was a member of the State Social Welfare Board from 1956 to 1961, when she guided the Board members in running the Project Implementation Committees in her own Zone—Bankura and Purulia districts—which were the first to have *pucca* buildings as community centres for women.

She started a dai[36] training centre at Bankura Clinic and had trained three successive batches of dais who were available for social welfare projects. She would not rest till each one of them was absorbed. It was a mission for her to accomplish an assignment. She could never rest until she was able to complete the job she took up as her own.

She had been the founder and honorary Secretary of the AIWC's Calcutta Branch, when Charulata Mukherjee was the President in 1927. She continued her connection with AIWC till the last day of her life, and continued to inspire us with patriotic songs of early days, sung in her melodious voice.

Later, if her failing health made her unable to function actively in an emergency situation, she would rope in all her friends and admirers and infuse in them her spirit and zeal for service. Words of encouragement and appreciation were generously given to the juniors, who will cherish them forever and will remember her with gratitude.

All India Women's Conference,
Calcutta Metropolitan Branch,
***Report* 1981-82, pp. 11-12**

[36] Dai = midwife.

The welcoming smile

Remembering Ashoka-di

Remembering Saibal and Partha, 2002

Ashoka-di, A Tribute

Jasodhara Bagchi

A friend's mother is always *Mashima*. Then why is it that Partha's mother was Ashoka-di to me? A very interesting answer came from the African-American writer Alice Walker:

> We are together, my child and I, mother and child, yes, but sisters, really against whatever denies all that we are.

This is the sisterhood, as part of which I would like to celebrate the memory of the wonderful lady that Ashoka Gupta was.

All her friends, relatives and admirers gathered here today will remember many public events and achievements in the public-spirited life of our Ashoka-di. Yet others will talk about the many private acts for which she will remain memorable. I would like to begin my personal tribute through the mother-child dyad with which I had begun. Because the area that held me captive to Ashoka-di was the special relationship between Ashoka-di and her mother Jyotirmoyee Debi.

Not many people will know that it was due to Ashoka-di's personal intervention that the School of Women's Studies, Jadavpur University, received its formal sanction from the UGC. One of the things that had interested her about our proposal was my vision of reprinting the nearly forgotten writings of women writers of Bengal, many of whom were victims of collective amnesia in the mainstream of Bangla writing. Of course, Jyotirmoyee Debi was high up on my list, and after we started formally with the work, Jyotirmoyee Debi was the second author whom we took up. Behind the volume with the red cover designed by late Raghunath Goswami and edited by late Subir Roy Choudhury with able assistance from Abhijit Sen, there were stretches of long and intensive search and selection from the writings of her mother that Ashoka-di had stored with so much love and care. We discovered that it was she who had sent in her mother's first writing for publication, and thereby launched this remarkable writer on her long journey. This is the mother-child dyad that Alice Walker celebrated in which the mother is saved by the child from oblivion. To quote Alice Walker again:

> It is not my child who has purged my face from history and her story and left my story just that, a mystery; my child loves my face and would have it on every page, if she could, as I have loved my own parents above all others...

It was while working with her on her mother's writings that Subir Roy Choudhury, the editor of our series and a friend of her son Partha Sarathi Gupta, tried to persuade Ashoka-di that she should focus on her own life and write. So you will realise how happy we were in Jadavpur Unversity when Ashoka-di's Noakhali book came out, although Subirbabu did not live to see it. Years later, in 2005, appeared her own memoir, a remarkable joint effort by the author with Sipra Bhattacharya and Ranjana Das Gupta. Ashoka-di's was a full life lived both inside and outside home. A remarkable homemaker, she brought up four high-achieving children following the ideology of a joint family. As visitors to her house we have always been given something to eat appropriate to the time of the day that we visited her. Each item would have her personal touch in choice and preparation. Only a few days before she died, I went to say goodbye to her before going away on a holiday to Cambridge, her granddaughter Niharika and she were there to receive me. Of course, the usual delicious food and fruit was brought in as it was in the morning that I visited her.

That was the occasion when I witnessed yet again how unbureaucratic her informal network of social work had been. A neighbour came and she put forward her requirements to her, knowing her to be a generous donor. In return, she made arrangements to admit a lady known to the neighbour in the short-stay home in Rajpur with which she was closely associated. This was the simple spirit of give and take in which she conducted intricate processes of catering to the want of women and children in need.

I had occasion to share her involvement with the activities of the All India Women's Conference (AIWC) when Ashoka-di and Phulrenu-di wanted me to be the Chairperson of the Reception Committee of the AIWC annual conference to be held in Kolkata in 2006. She was there in meetings before and after the conference, to discuss what needed to be done. What was most amazing, however, was that at the age of 94 not only did she attend in her wheelchair the entire inaugural programme, but stayed back for the seminar we had organised on Women and Personal Laws. It is then that I witnessed her stamina in supporting public causes for women.

Shortly before her death, she personally accompanied the Secretary of the Kasturba Trust when, on my appeal to the Governor, they kindly opened a crèche for working mothers in Panchannagram which had been devastated by a terrible fire.

She would often ask us in the Women's Commission to help distressed women when they needed help to negotiate any difficult situation. The most memorable were the efforts she had put in for the poor woman and her family who had looked after Smt Renuka Ray and her son when they were dying and who were about to be deprived of their dues by some rich men. With her by our side, the Women's Commission fought tooth and nail to see what could be retrieved on their behalf. Her involvement with the women's movement certainly helped her to overcome the public/private divide in which so many of our lives are caught. I have sometimes wondered whether it was this involvement that gave her the strength to continue with her work despite the tragic and untimely passing of her eldest child Professor Partha Sarathi Gupta, and that of her eldest daughter Dr Shakuntala Dasgupta. We had further evidence of this when she helped us put together our first book on 'Gender and Partition in Eastern India'. As she was a contributor herself, we could not dedicate the book to her. Reading between lines, however, our dedication was really meant for her.

The West Bengal Commission was specially proud of Smt Ashoka Gupta. In June 2002, along with Smt Maya Niyogi, then Chairperson of the Social Welfare Advisory Board, the Commission organised a special Reception for Ashoka-di, who had herself been the Chairperson of the West Bengal Social Welfare Advisory Board. She was resplendent, and the main tribute to her was read by Smt Bindu Zutshi, the then Member-Secretary of the West Bengal Commission for Women, who, as her daughter Kasturi's batchmate, had enjoyed a lot of her personal affection. In 2007, I was very happy when, as the Chairperson of the Women's Commission, my nomination was accepted and Smt Ashoka Gupta received the prestigious Jamnalal Bajaj Award for her outstanding work among the women of India. In 2007, I, as a former teacher of Jadavpur University, felt proud when Ashoka-di was given D.Litt *Honoris Causa* by my University. My only regret was that, since I had retired, I was not entrusted with writing the citation.

My husband and my younger daughter have received Ashoka-di's affection, just as I had done. I look upon Kasturi as a younger sister. I hope the entire family with such a wonderful *mater familias* draws inspiration from her personality, spirit and dedication. And when I say her family, I cannot help thinking that I mean a great deal of not just West Bengal but of the rest of India.

Ashoka-di, Anecdotes and their Afterlives

Sarmistha Dutta Gupta

Last night there was a hailstorm. Today a near-cyclone is ripping through this island in Sunderban where I have been camping these last few days. I come here often as part of a voluntary organisation that has been trying to work with school communities towards making schools gender-just spaces. If you wonder what this could possibly have to do with remembering Ashoka-di, I won't keep you waiting long.

For a couple of years now in a gram panchayat in Sunderban we have been holding discussions and workshops, legal awareness camps and film festivals in collaboration with a high school, on issues related to gender and sexuality. Just as we are thrilled that our pedagogic work has triggered the emergence of a new local group on the island—a group that has actively started campaigning against marriage of adolescents and other social issues—we are at the same time plagued with uncertainty. Starved of funds, we are not sure how long we can continue our work through members' contributions. We have been pleading with a leading Indian agency for funds for over a year. In spite of their enthusiasm with our detailed proposal, the nationally-renowned agency recently told us that they may not be able to support our work because they are trying hard to converge to a 'programmatic mode.' Though empowering adolescent girls is high on the priority list of this agency, in order to be considered for funding, organisations not only have to match the agency's priorities but also have to adopt its programmatic mode. This is by no means unique and I am sure both voluntary and professionally managed NGOs very often have to face the difficult choice of catering to local needs and priorities on the one hand and the programme priorities set by donor bodies on the other.

I often remember Ashoka-di when I think of 'development' and the politics of funding in our part of the world today. Actually it brings to mind one of the numerous anecdotes that she had shared with me when I used to visit her in connection with my research on a gendered history of politics in late-colonial Bengal. We would often talk about contemporary issues and one day, while discussing the question of funding, she told me what the eminent Sarvodaya worker Malati Devi Choudhury had told her once. Malati Devi and Ashoka Gupta were attending a high-profile conference of social workers and policy-makers in Delhi. At the end of the first day's proceedings, Malati Devi summed it up by telling Ashoka-di, 'Have you figured out what this is all about? If you are working in a village that badly needs tubewells, they would lure you with funds to build roads there. If you decide to apply for the money and build a road where you think it is needed most, they might even tell you how the road should be routed. Soon you will find your agenda is being completely dictated by what they are funding.' This story dates back to the mid-1980s when the funded NGO boom was not yet upon us. Essays like Arundhati Roy's 'Help that Hinders' took another twenty years to come. But the likes of Malati Devi Chowdhury, with a lifetime's experience in social work, were quick to figure out and resist the politics of neo-liberal funding that would make NGOs accountable primarily to their funders and not to the people they work with. I also learnt from Ashoka-di that Malati Devi refused to accept the Jamnalal Bajaj Award from the hands of a prime minister who, she believed, had done nothing to propagate Gandhian values.

Conversations with Ashoka-di not only yielded such rare vignettes about her predecessors and contemporaries but also showed her deep engagement with present issues. Ashoka Gupta herself was deeply interested in the nature of work that NGOs with professionally trained social workers do today and the kind of voluntary social work she had done all her life. When Ashoka-di joined social work in the late 1930s, Sarojini Naidu and other leading women active in public life were calling out to young women of their class to make full use of their education and 'feminine' qualities beyond the confines of domesticity. Most of the women who responded to this call successfully combined philanthropy with domesticity and applied a woman's skill in home management to managing the larger family outside. Ashoka Gupta was one of them. It may be worthwhile to recall here that she was a student of mathematics at Bethune College and only a couple of months before her BSc examination was married to Saibal Kumar Gupta, an ICS officer. She left Calcutta for her marital home in Barisal in East Bengal and could come back to stay with her mother and prepare for her final examination only ten days before it was to start. In spite of this, she did fairly well and scored the highest marks in chemistry. Within a couple of years of her marriage she had begun taking charge of the elaborate affairs of a close-knit joint family, including complex weddings, and she has written about how she honed her skills as an organiser through shouldering such family responsibilities.

In her memoirs, among illuminating episodes on the early years of AIWC work, the Bengal Famine, the Noakhali riots and refugee rehabilitation, I find the chapter 'Reflections on Social Work' extremely relevant to present debates on the role of the NGOs in addressing social inequalities. Not that I agree with everything she says. In particular, I often disagreed with the way she glorified unpaid social work. She always took great pride in the fact that at AIWC not only did they never take any money for the work they did, but also paid for their travel and other actual expenses. She was averse to the idea of community workers/social workers getting paid for their work. I would retort by giving her examples from real life. What of the woman whose husband runs a small grocery store, and who is struggling hard to have her two daughters complete school? Suppose she is working for an organisation that counsels and provides legal aid to women who have been victims of different kinds of violence. For all you know her modest salary may be helping her daughters' education. Her class position is different from yours, I would say, and the fact that she is a paid worker does not make her any less equal.

If you have to have as members/decision-makers only people who can afford to fully volunteer their services and pay for their travel etc, your organisation is bound to be an elitist one. Ashoka-di would relent for the time being but soon she would come up with other examples to underscore the problems arising out of treating a social worker's job as a time-bound or a salary-bound one. I tried to reason with her that it ultimately boils down to one's commitment and interest in the work. It is unfair to think that a paid worker would lack commitment or that an honorary worker may necessarily be free of vested interests.

Ashoka-di combined a fervent commitment to her work with an innate interest in people—be it a brother-in-law's grandniece or a gardener's son or an inmate of a shelter-home or a celebrity writer. She had all their personal details at her fingertips and if she knew that you and she had any common acquaintance, she would surely ask you for an update while offering a sumptuous snack before you began talking to her about work. Information about people and events—not always the kind that one is likely to find in public records—were stored both in her computer-like brain as well as in her personal archive. This archive included a range of documents: old newsletters brought out by social welfare organisations, news clippings that may have been of interest to her, correspondence with a wide range of people, diaries, manuscripts of her mother's writings, reports of inspection tours she undertook may be fifty years ago, books written by fellow social workers or books gifted to her by historians—the list is endless. Facsimile of letters written to her by people in Noakhali in 1946-47 that have been included in the present volume, should give the reader some idea of Ashoka Gupta the archivist. The letters she exchanged with her husband from the 1930s to the 1980s, one letter a day on average if either of them happened to be away from home, has been a treasure-trove to scholars working on the histories of marriage, companionship and intimacies in modern Bengal. Her entire collection is a rich but unconventional source of history, especially for those who, in the course of their research, have time and again found such unconventional sites—which yield written, oral as well as visual material—helping to breach the closures suggested by conventional ones. When I was exploring the emergence of different narratives of selfhood by women in twentieth century Bengal through the history of a few periodicals with different ideological moorings, it was imperative to search for such alternative sites of knowledge. And in this journey I was guided by archivists of a different order—archivists like Ashoka Gupta and Kamala Dasgupta and Kanak Mukherjee who cared to preserve and remember what institutions like libraries, archives and museums had obliterated.

Let me end by sharing with you an anecdote that epitomises how the public and the private came together in her papers, as it did in all aspects of her life. One evening about ten-twelve years ago I was sitting with Ashoka-di, with a trunk full of papers she had treasured for more than sixty years spread out before us. Most of her passionate acquisition dated back to 1946-48—pertaining to the Noakhali riots and Partition—and among other things there was a bunch of old letters. One of the letters that still rings in my ears was from her daughter Shakuntala, who had written from Chittagong to to her mother in Noakhali, begging Ashoka to come back home so that she could see her just once. Ashoka-di was working in the Noakhali camps and had not seen her family for some time. Only her infant daughter Kasturi was with her. The older daughter Shakuntala promised her mother never ever to disobey her if she came home once. '*Ma, tomar duti paye pori, ekbar bari esho,*' ('Ma, I fall at your feet [and beg you] to come home just once') was, I think, her appeal. As Ashoka-di and I were talking about what it meant to be separated from her family and working in Noakhali after the 1946 riots, I fished out another postcard—this time not written by any of her family or associates. It was from a young boy to his father, sometime in 1947-48. The boy, almost the same age as Shakuntala, had written to his father but did not know to what address the letter should be posted because his father was lost in post-Partition violence. He did not even know whether his father was dead or alive but imagined that he would see him some day. The boy wanted to know how he was to be reunited again with his father. I asked Ashoka-di where she had found the letter and why she had kept it. She told me it was written by one of the inmates of an ashram she was associated with and the boy had asked her to post the letter. Ashoka-di had treasured the letter all these years because she could not throw away such a poignant plea from a child to his parent—a child who had lost his father to the country's Partition forever. Whenever I think of Ashoka-di, this is what flashes across my mind first and I begin to understand her life's work and why her memoirs, *In the Path of Service,* is one of the most passionate yet unsentimental accounts of India's Partition that I have ever read.

Ashoka-di

Moushami Sengupta

Amidst all my work and worries, I often go down memory lane and think about Ashoka-di. I met her for the first time at Baroma's house at Entally, Kolkata. Gradually, my involvement in social work brought me close to her. I joined the Loka Seva Samity (Khirpai, West Bengal). This had been created by two remarkable people, Annadaprasad Chaudhury and his wife Hiranbala Chaudhury (Baroma). They had been close to Ashoka-di and her husband Sri Saibal Gupta from long before Independence. Ashoka-di was the President of many organisations—SOS Children's Village, Mahila Seva Samity, Buniyadi Vidyapith, Indian Society for Sponsorship and Adoption, and Ananda-Ashram, among others. Loka Seva Samity was one of them. What differentiated it from the others was that it was a rural project in a tribal belt, very near Birsingha village, the birthplace of the eminent social reformer Iswar Chandra Vidyasagar.

In the years that she was President of All India Women's Conference (1986 to 1990), she opened a short-stay home at Khirpai that gave shelter to destitute women. The first batch was of 18 women with their children from the Liluah Home. Most of them were mentally disturbed, their children malnourished. Under Ashoka-di's guidance, we managed to bring the difficult situation under control. Later we sent the children to the Cottage Scheme at Sarsuna, Behala. Today they have grown up to be useful citizens. Mahila Seva Samity, under the auspices of the Government of India, followed the same kind of programme.

Ashoka-di was one of the founder members of the All-India Committee for the Eradication of Illiteracy among Women. Its headquarters was at Sarojini House, New Delhi. I worked for the Bengal Branch till 2010. Adult education reached new heights in the Beleghata area of Kolkata as a high literacy rate was recorded among the mothers of the students studying in Buniyadi Bidyapith. Ashoka-di was President of this school, to which she was emotionally very attached. She continued to raise funds for this school till her last breath. Ashoka-di strongly believed in women's empowerment. Under her patronage, a fair, 'WOMEN 88' was organised in Kolkata by Swayambhar; the next year a Craft Bazaar was held at the Kolkata Maidan. I enjoyed working with them. Our handicrafts workers from Khirpai brought mats and tools to Kolkata for the fairs. The buyers appreciated the handicrafts and became aware of the talent that lay hidden in our villages.

In 1989, Ashoka-di sent some AIWC members, including me, to Bhubaneswar, for a UNIFEM leadership training camp. It was a great experience. She joined us there later. From there Ashoka-di, Reba Ray and I went to Puri, where Ashoka-di had a meeting with the Puri branch of the AIWC regarding short-stay homes. For me personally, this training was a turning-point—it helped me rediscover myself as a social worker. In December, 1990, the annual conference of AIWC took place at Hastings House in Kolkata. Shobhana Ranade was elected President, succeeding Ashoka-di. The counting of votes took place in the campus of Hastings House till midnight under Ashoka-di's supervision. It had been a very hectic day for her, and for me a vivid memory is that she saw to it that all the workers were given hot tomato soup on that cold winter night.

On the afternoon of December 6, 1992, I went to Ashoka-di's house for some work. There had been a tragic death in her family, and she was naturally very disturbed, but she went on working. Mr SN Menon, her son-in-law (and the Chief Minister's private secretary) entered the room and told us that the Babri Masjid had been demolished and that curfew had been imposed in Kolkata and adjacent areas. I finished my work and rushed home. On the days that followed, lootings and killings occurred in different localities of Kolkata–Tyangra, Park Circus, Dhobi

Ghat, Pilkhana, and Khidirpur. Hundreds of slums were burnt down. We, the members of Mahila Seva Samity, sought permission from the local thana to carry out relief work under Ashoka-di's guidance. We collected milk powder, rice flakes, jaggery, clothes, medicines and ORS to distribute among the victims, who had taken shelter at Bengal Potteries on Convent Road and in some school buildings. The Deputy Inspector-General, Information Bureau, helped us, especially with transport. The season being winter, I remember, we bought 100 blankets from Borobazar and distributed them among the women and children. The Ramakrishna Mission supplied mid-day meals. One day, Geeta Mukherjee, MP, a distinguished member of the CPI, came to see our work. She recalled how Ashoka-di had taught her swimming many years ago, when they were in East Bengal!

One day in 1993, Reba Ray anxiously called me from a nursing home asking me to go to Imphal to solve some problems regarding short-stay homes. Manipur, especially Imphal, was going through turbulence. She had been expected to go but could not, as her husband had just suffered a heart attack. Ashoka-di had suggested to her that I must go. I went to Ashoka-di's house to find her waiting for me with files and air-tickets, and a warm coat! Manipur being a cold place, the coat really helped.

In 1995, I was expecting my first child, some years after my marriage. She invited some members of the Lok Seva Samity to her house for lunch to celebrate the occasion. On the day of my baby shower, there was a violent cyclone. Few of the invited people turned up. To my surprise, in spite of the terrible weather, Ashoka-di came to my house with Arati Srimal, and with a beautiful saree for me. She had lunch with me and spent almost the whole day at my house.

I had a small publication unit called Upama. In 1999, I was fortunate enough to be able to publish the Bengali version of Smt Lakshmi Sehgal's autobiography. Dr Jasodhara Bagchi wrote the Foreword to the book. It was released at Bangla Academy, in the presence of Dr Sisir Bose, Ashoka-di, Smt Lakshmi Sehgal and many other personalities. Ashoka-di chaired the book release.

Ashoka-di was a great human being who stood by anyone in need or on a selfless mission. Anu Bandopadhyay, an eminent Gandhian

With Moushami Sengupta, 2005

leader, had an unusual relationship with Ashoka-di. She used to knit woollen mufflers and scarves, and sell them to NGOs like ours. She herself used to wear hand-woven pajama-kurtas and walk barefoot. Sometimes she used to get so angry with the evils of society that she refused to eat for days. She once broke her fast at Ashoka-di's house, after eating a bowl of payesh in the presence of Tara Gandhi, Gandhiji's granddaughter. When Gopalkrishna Gandhi came to Kolkata as the Governor, Ashoka-di requested him to meet Anu Bandopadhyay, then on her deathbed.

I recall how, in May 2008, she was very weak and tired. But she called me and asked me to come to Raj Bhavan for a programme. I went to her house, where she was anxiously waiting in her wheelchair for her granddaughter. Niharika came quickly from her workplace, and the three of us went to Raj Bhavan together. It was my last journey with her. On July 8, she took her last breath.

How can I describe what Ashoka-di means to me? She was my inspiration in the form of a philosopher and guide. Words cannot express the love and respect I have for my guru. I lived twenty-three years under her tutelage and still continue to live like that. Innumerable memories come to mind as I think of her. What I have written is just a drop of water in the ocean.

Ashoka Gupta

Kasturi Gupta Menon

My mother was only 5 1/2 years old when her father Kiron Chandra Sen died. An up-and-coming lawyer in Bankipur (near Patna), he fell a victim to the influenza epidemic which had swept through the country in the aftermath of the First World War.

Her mother's father—Shri Abinash Chandra Sen—was the owner of a *jagir* (estate) in the princely state of Jaipur where he was a Cabinet Minister to the then Maharaja. It was *he* who came and took charge of his young widowed daughter and her family of six little children and took them back with him to Rajasthan. And so, leaving behind the moorings of her stable childhood, Ma and her siblings travelled back with their grandfather all the way to distant Jaipur.

Although her Dadamoshai's enormous Jaipur house was comfortable, they felt lost, as she recalls, 'In a totally different milieu'. Ma's older sister and brother (Amiya and Arun) had been going to school in Patna, which had had to be discontinued when they moved to Jaipur. It was only when a decision was taken to send Ma and Arun to Delhi to continue their studies there, that some form of stability again re-entered her life.

Ma's formal education began in Delhi in 1919 with her admission to the Indraprastha School when she was just six years old. In those days girls from Hindu families were rarely sent to school as it was felt that knowledge of household skills was all that they needed to acquire. It was her mother (Jyotirmoyee Debi) however, who had insisted that

'Ashoka must accompany Arun', thereby displaying a wisdom and foresight both rare and exceptional.

Her granduncle's house in Delhi (where she now began to live) exposed her to a different world. His house was in Chandni Chowk, facing the Parade Ground where, in those days, all processions and political meetings took place. She vividly remembers the day when Swami Shraddhanand defied the British in Chandni Chowk during the Rowlatt Satyagraha, and, 'how Gandhiji arrived flanked by the two leaders of the Khilafat Movement'. Nationalist fervour swept through their lives and the older women discarded their fashionable saris for coarser handloom ones. She was privy to all the political discussions among the elders, even though she was at that time all of 7 or 8 years old!

In 1922 Ma moved to Calcutta with her brother Arun, to attend the wedding of her older sister Amiya who had turned 13! After a long time the family, including all the younger siblings who had been left behind in Jaipur, were together again.

Admission to Duff School and later to St Margaret's followed. Alongside came the exposure to books and magazines such as *Mouchak, Sishusathi, Jadughar* and *Sandesh,* and popular journals such as *Probashi, Sabujpatra, Bharatbarsha* and *Shanibarer Chithi.* In short, it was an intellectually stimulating environment where the youngsters were encouraged to think and read. A few years later Ma appeared for her matriculation examination and stood 1st among the girls and achieved 'letter marks' in both her Mathematics papers, and in Bengali and Sanskrit.

It was during this period that she also came to be exposed to all kinds of debates. Women were emerging from the confines of their homes, and discussing the Hindu Code Bill, and meetings about the Rights of Women were being held. There was a churning in society, and new ideas and thoughts were being articulated. It was this intellectual stimulus to which she was exposed in her girlhood and adolescence both in Delhi and Calcutta, and the 'fractured quality' of her childhood, that shaped her character and stood her in good stead to withstand all kinds of upheavals that she had to face later—including the trauma of Partition.

As children we always enjoyed listening to Ma recounting the story of how Baba courted her! A loving but strict father, and a stern disciplinarian, we found it hard to imagine him as a young eligible bachelor! 'Your father was brought to our house by "Panchumama", who had met him when he was posted as sub-divisional officer in Contai. He had expressed an interest in meeting Ma (Jyotirmoyee Debi) whose essays and stories he had read in contemporary Bengali journals like *Prabashi* and *Sabuj Patra.*'

'One visit during the Puja vacation was followed by a second, and a second by a third. This was followed by three more visits during the Christmas break. It was during one of these meetings that he asked me whether I had read Bertrand Russell!'

'And what did you say?' we would chorus. ' "Not Bertrand Russell," ' I had replied,' she said. ' "But I have read Thomas Hardy, Lytton Strachey and DH Lawrence." ' A formidable list indeed for a young Maths undergraduate at Bethune College!

A 'Ghoti-Bangaal' marriage in those days was an exception rather than the rule and theirs was all the more so as it had been 'arranged'. And even though she adjusted beautifully to her husband's huge joint family across the sweeping Padma, she retained her own cultural identity always.

Ma's marriage with Baba took place in April 1933 and with that began her life as a civilian's wife. After Baba's stint in Contai, he was transferred from the Executive branch of the ICS to the Judicial side, and it was as the District Judge's wife that Ma travelled with him to Faridpur, Dhaka, Krishnanagar, Rajshahi, Bankura and Jessore.

It was in Dhaka that she first came in contact with a number of women's organisations—(a) the All-India Women's Conference (AIWC), (b) the Ananda Ashram, (c) National Conference of Women in India (NCWI) and (d) the Dipali Sangha.

It was in Dhaka also that she was first drawn into co-ordinating a fund-raising programme for all these women's organisations. And it was in Dhaka that she became a member of the AIWC.

She speaks (in her memoirs) of having learnt a number of lessons from this experience: That, 'dividing the work-load puts less pressure on individuals'; ...'when many groups work together a greater body of talent can be tapped'; and, 'exposure to the under-privileged sections of society revealed the innumerable skills that these women possessed'. Imperceptibly, she had begun to learn the skills of man-management that she would find so useful in her work later.

In 1938 Baba left for England to study for the Bar, and she returned to Calcutta to attend her brother Arun's marriage. She took the opportunity to attend the historic Congress session which was held in Calcutta that year and where Subhas Bose was elected Congress President. She witnessed the drama that followed his resignation immediately thereafter. Although she was never a member of any political party, she took keen interest in what was happening in the surcharged political atmosphere.

But by 1939 war clouds had begun to loom over Europe, and the British Government curtailed Baba's leave and directed him to report for duty back to India. Baba's posting to Jessore, and later to Krishnanagore were like a brief interlude for them, the last days before the sun finally set on the Raj.

Gandhiji's 'Quit India' call of 1942 coincided with Baba's transfer as District Judge, Bankura. The World War was in its third year but the gentle hilly terrain of Bankura—green after a good monsoon—seemed so serene and peaceful. There was no sign at all of the famine that would ravage the district and the state in the following months.

The first signs were an imperceptible drifting of a few families towards Bankura town. Then the numbers began to swell, and soon whole villages were migrating from the countryside—pregnant women, starving children, many of whom had not eaten for days. Under the leadership of Mrs Usha Haldar (the then Commissioner's wife), and through the Bankura branch of the AIWC, gruel kitchens were opened and 'khichuri' served to the famished women and children, as the men had migrated in search of work elsewhere. The famine relief work in Bankura was Ma's baptism into active social work. In her own words, 'This work gave me great satisfaction, joy, and brought peace to my mind. At last I had found a sense of direction. I had found my path.'

I was born in December 1944, when they were posted in Bankura. I was ten years younger than my brother Partha and seven years younger than my sister Shakuntala (Kunta). Five months later Baba was again transferred—this time as District Judge to Chittagong—and the family journeyed by train, steamer and by train again to the easternmost flank of what was then still known as East Bengal.

Chittagong was bustling with jeeps, soldiers and army personnel when they finally arrived, as the town was very close to the war-front. Food and clothes were still scarce and rationed.

In 1946 communal trouble began to ferment and stories of the abduction of Hindu girls began to filter in, which flared up in Noakhali in the form of riots. Hindu families were fleeing their villages, and relief camps under the AIWC's different branches were set up. Ma's services were once again enlisted, and she plunged wholeheartedly into reaching relief material to the affected areas. Noakhali, which was hit the worst, was declared out of bounds by Mr Carter, the Divisional Commissioner, and remained so until the Congress President, Acharya Kripalani, expressed a wish to visit Chittagong. After Acharya Kripalani's visit, access to Noakhali was allowed.

Gandhiji reached Chandpur in November 1946. He directed the relief workers to go and live in the affected villages, 'For courage, like fear was contagious', and the presence of relief workers would give confidence to the terror-stricken villagers. Ma was keen to go, but had *me* to consider—then just one and a half years old. I would obviously have to be left behind. She was on the horns of a dilemma. Gandhiji solved the problem in his inimitable way by suggesting that she take me along. And so I accompanied her when she finally left Chittagong for Tumchar camp.

Ma's Noakhali exposure was a watershed in her life—a hands-on experience that would stand her in good stead forever after. Among the many lessons learnt from Gandhiji was his passion for cleanliness;

his insistence on punctuality (which he would enforce through his famous pocket watch!); his frugal spartan meals, and his total commitment to a secular India.

And so the months passed. So focused was Ma on her relief work, that she failed to hear the distant knell of the partition lines being drawn up, until Baba himself was summoned to Calcutta to work for the Partition Committee later in the year. And so with a heavy heart, after a year and a half at Noakhali, Ma returned to Chittagong. Boxes were packed, furniture crated, friends and colleagues bade farewell to, some perhaps forever.

My own memories of Chittagong are sepia images of a distant past. Of a red-brick two-storeyed bungalow flanked by a long marble verandah; of a hand-cranked HMV gramophone standing in the lobby at the head of the stairs with its stack of 78″ rpm records; of a pebbled beach at Cox's Bazaar; and the echo of the 'Raghupati Raghava' refrain to which I would lend my shrill treble during evening prayers at the camp.

Partition and After

I was perhaps 3½ years old when we finally reached Calcutta.

The house opposite the Calcutta race-course was a sprawling two-storeyed mansion with 12 to 16 rooms and two 40 feet-long verandahs. It was flanked on one side by the Lower Circular road, and had a rambling garden with mango and jackfruit trees and a vegetable patch at the rear. The house was so large that any number of cousins and their parents could be accommodated. East Bengal had become East Pakistan, and all Baba's brothers and sisters (except for the eldest), had migrated to Calcutta. 'The house was like a boarding house where a wedding party had assembled', to quote Ma's own words. I had a cot in my parents' bedroom upstairs which also included a partioned-off portion of the 40 feet-long verandah. One day, to my delight I came upon a pair of high-heeled open-toed navy blue sandals resting below Ma's 'alna'. I was most surprised as I had never seen her wear fashionable footwear or even 'dress up'. I put my tiny feet into them and lurched out into the verandah.

'May I have these when I grow up?' I had asked. 'Yes, of course,' she had answered with a smile. 'I have only worn them once.'

Ma's side of the dressing table (which she shared with Baba) always had a 'Jessore' comb, a bottle of Jabakusum hair-oil, a wooden sindur pot, and a jar of 'Afghan Snow' (equivalent to today's 'Fair and Lovely'), which she used only when she went to wedding receptions with my father. A gift of a tiny bottle of 'Evening in Paris' perfume was hidden in the deep recesses of a drawer!

By early 1948 streams of refugees from Punjab had started to arrive in Calcutta, and Ma again became immersed in relief and rehabilitation work. Bales of jungle-green merino wool were gifted from Australia for knitting garments for the displaced families. For lack of space, some of these were stacked on the 40 feet verandah on the ground floor, among which I recall playing hide-and-seek with a girl cousin a few months younger.

An army of volunteers would come every day to take away a measured portion of yarn. These would be returned in three or four days in the form of sweaters, socks or caps. Gradually Ma found herself drawn inexorably into the rehabilitation programmes for the Punjab and Bengali refugees. The latter came to India in waves, in 1948, 1950, 1953 and later, a continuous influx that never seemed to end, and which reached its peak in 1964 following communal riots in East Pakistan. It was at this juncture that she also came in contact with women from other communities—Gujarati, Marwari, Malayali, Assamese, Sikh and Punjabi—and with whom she remained friends right until the end. The Mahila Seva Samity was set up around this time.

Ma's other great love was the Girl Guide movement with which she had been associated since her Duff School days. Through our school, Didi (Kunta) and I were members of the 'Bulbul' and Girl Guide troops, and enjoyed the camps and jamborees to which we were sent. And it was as the State Commissioner for Guides that Ma herself went abroad for the first time—to the United States, at the invitation of the International Headquarters for Guides.

After she returned from her four-month sojourn in the United States, we found certain innovations creeping into our family meals. A 'salad' became a mandatory accompaniment with dinner, and we were often served homemade 'hamburgers' when we returned from school at 3.00 p.m. I became the proud owner of a stiff 'can-can' underskirt (which was then the rage), which was the envy of the girls in my class. Picture-post cards of the Grand Canyon, the Red Wood forests, and the Niagara Falls—in fact from wherever she travelled in the United States—lit up our lives.

By the mid-fifties she was appointed Chairman of the State Social Welfare Board, which had an office on Free School Street very close to New Market. It was also close to the Girl Guide office on Kyd Street to which we often walked after school to meet her. Baba had taken over as Chairman of the Calcutta Improvement Trust, an assignment he enjoyed immensely and with which he stayed until he retired.

Dandakaranya

Baba retired from service in 1962, and was appointed Chairman of the Dandakaranya Development Authority (DDA) in November the following year. Dada (Partha) had returned from Oxford but left to join Delhi University, and Didi got married soon after. I was an

"Ma's other great love was the Girl Guide movement", 1955 photograph

undergraduate at Presidency College, and Apala, the youngest, was still in school—there being almost a ten -year gap between the two of us.

Ma joined Baba in Dandakaranya leaving Apala and me behind in Calcutta. The communal riots in East Pakistan had triggered a fresh flood of migration of Hindu families to India, all of whom were herded off to DDA's Mana Transit Camp. The temperature had peaked to 40 degrees, and water and basic amenities were scarce. The condition of the camp and its inmates was appalling, and Delhi, so far away from reality, was slow to react. Since Ma was a member of the Central Social Welfare Board (CSWB), she was able to enlist the help of voluntary organisations such as the Indian Red Cross Society, the Social Welfare Boards, and Gandhi Gram. Her work, as she herself has described, 'Was both official and unofficial'. She would accompany Dr Bhupen Rakshit Ray (a former revolutionary and social worker), and also Dr Shankar Ghosh-Dastidar (the camp's medical officer), on their rounds in order to assess the ground realities for herself. Her efforts to open schools and make life more meaningful for the displaced people have been described in her memoirs.

Perhaps what hurt her most was the Centre's total lack of sensitivity to the problem. 'The government's DDA policy not only lacked materially but also fell short of understanding the psychological and human needs of the refugees', she was to write. Things came to such a pass that Baba could no longer continue to function effectively, and had perforce to resign. Ma always felt she had not completed her work in Dandakaranya, and although she and Baba had come away, she always devised ways by which to remain in touch.

Gradually Ma's sphere of activities had expanded with her nomination to the Central Social Welfare Board (CSWB). This gave her the scope to visit other states such as Tripura, Assam, Orissa and Rajasthan, and also to assist in the formulation of policy through the Ministries of Rehabilitation and Social Welfare.

She visited Brazil in 1962 as a part of a three-member delegation to review the working of the Youth Club programmes, and later went again to the USA and Japan. Wherever she went she would post us beautiful picture postcards, and occasionally bring back gifts of 'makeup'. I was once even gifted an 'itsy-bitsy' two-piece purple swimsuit with white polka dots!

Her encouragement when I decided to sit for the Civil Services examination was a source of immense support which gave me the courage to dare. Each one of us felt that to her he/she was the child that was special, and I am sure Dada, Didi and Apala would have the same story to tell.

She set up the Indian Society for Sponsorship and Adoption in 1975, and was involved with the SOS Children's Village programme, of which she was President until the end. She was nominated to the Life Insurance Corporation Board for two terms, and elected President of the AIWC in 1986—an organisation of which she had been a member for many decades.

The Jamnalal Bajaj Award given to her in November 2007 for her lifetime work with women and children, and the *D.Litt* awarded to her by Jadavpur University in December of the same year, were a source of deep delight. The money from the former was immediately set aside to build an additional floor for Buniyadi Vidyapith, a school

Family gathering at Guptipara, at the ancestral home of Ashoka's father Kiron Chandra Sen, Durga Puja 1997. Kasturi is second from the right in the front row

Aabaar esho!—*the familiar smiling farewell*

for underprivileged children, and to the Mahila Seva Samity for constructing additional bathrooms for an Old Age Home for women in Rajpur.

'Write something about Ashoka-di,' I was told. 'Not about her public work, but what she was like as a mother.' But the two strands were so entwined that I could not separate them.

'I will write a piece about her within four pages,' I told myself, as I sat down with pen and paper. But how does one encapsulate ninety years and more in a four-page span? How does one capture the fun and the light and the laughter which enriched our growing years, and lingered on like an afterglow right until the last?

'Strong feisty personalities like her come seldom into our lives,' as Mrs Reyhan Dutta, a former colleague from the SOS recalled, 'and when they do, they make a deep impression. She was one of a kind—they don't make them like her anymore!'

Written for the Memorial Meeting for Ashoka Gupta, Kolkata, August 9, 2008

I wish to acknowledge Ashoka Gupta's *In the Path of Service* for details of chronology.

Glossary

akhra	(Hindi *akhara*) lit. wrestling site, also a place for assembly
alna	wooden stand for clothes
alur-dum	small whole potatoes cooked slowly in a spicy sauce
anchal	part of the sari which is draped over the shoulder and also used to cover the head
Babu	(used in eastern India) prefix/suffix to mean 'sir' or 'mister'
balak-balika	boys and girls
beyan	son's or daughter's in-laws
bonde	fried globules of gram-flour soaked in sugar syrup
boroma	older paternal uncle's wife
boro-didima	mother's maternal grandmother
boudi	older brother's wife
bustee	slum
Chandi Paath	(*Chandi* = the goddess Durga, *Paath* = reading), the ritual reading of the account of Durga's victory over the Asura king
chira	rice flakes
dai	midwife
darshan	audience
Devi/Debi	suffix for a woman's name, indicating respect
-di/didi	older sister
didima	mother's mother
Ghoti-Bangaal	*ghoti* = people originally of west Bengal, *bangaal* = people originally of east Bengal before the country's Partition, both somewhat derisory terms
gola	a conical granary
gosht	meat
gur	jaggery
jethima	wife of father's older brother
kamini	orange blossom, with an intoxicating fragrance
kantha	coverlet/quilt made up from old or torn saris
kanthi	a necklace of basil-seeds worn by Vaishnavs
khichuri	a hot dish of rice cooked with lentils and vegetables
khoi	puffed rice
kora	unbleached

kripa	kindness
luchi	light fried flour pancakes
Ma	mother
mamima	wife of mother's brother
markin	marking/Nankeen, strong machine-made cloth
mashi/mashima	mother's sister
maulabi	(Urdu *moulvi*) a learned Muslim/teacher
mehendi	henna
mez-di	second-eldest sister
mishti	sweetmeat
mite	a storage-area
muri	puffed rice
nabina	new/modern woman
paan	betel-leaf usually eaten after a meal/offered to guests
panjabi	(Hindi *kurta*) knee-length shirt worn by men
pathisapta	rice-flour pancake stuffed with sweetened coconut
payesh	rice cooked in sweetened milk
pishi	father's sister
poa	(Hindi *pav*) 1/4 *seer* (a *seer* being just a little more than a kilogram)
Podipishi	name of character in a famous children's book in Bengali by Lila Majumdar, used to mean an intellectual woman/blue-stocking
prachina	old/pre-modern woman
pucca	firm, used to describe buildings of brick rather than mud
puro	store-house
Rajsabha	royal court
Rangama	a form of addressing aunts or older women
roti	unleavened bread
sammelan	assembly
shamiana	cloth awning
sindur	vermilion powder applied along the parting in a woman's hair, to indicate she is married
Sm	abbreviation of Srimati, used as prefix for a respectable woman
than	a bolt of cloth
thamma	*thakurma,* father's mother
thana	police station
tuti	locket

Contributors

Jasodhara Bagchi, Professor Emeritus in the Department of Women's Studies, Jadavpur University, studied in Kolkata, Oxford and Cambridge. After teaching English Literature in Jadavpur University, she was the Founder-Director of the School of Women's Studies there. She is a founder-member of SACHETANA, and was Chairperson, West Bengal Commission for Women. Her range of interests include writings by women, nineteenth-century literature and intellectual history in England and Bengal, and Gender and Partition in Eastern India.

Kasturi Gupta Menon, Ashoka Gupta's second daughter, retired from the I.A.S. and is the Honorary President of the Crafts Council of India, a registered society which was set up by Kamaladevi Chattopadhyaya.

Moushami Sengupta did an M.A. in economics from Jadavpur University, and has been an active social worker. She worked closely with Ashoka Gupta in the Mahila Seva Samity and the AIWC.

Narayani Gupta, Ashoka Gupta's daughter-in-law, retired as professor of History, and is a consultant with INTACH.

Sarmistha Dutta Gupta, independent scholar, literary translator and an activist of the women's movement, is the author of *Identities and Histories: Women's Writing and Politics in Bengal* (2010), *Shantisudha Ghoser Nirbachito Rachana Sangraha* (Selected Works of Shantisudha Ghosh; 2008) and *Pather Ingit: Nirbachito Sambad-Samayikpatrey Bangali Meyer Samajbhavna* (Women, Print Culture and Social Change in Bengal; 2007). She is the founder-secretary of a Kolkata-based voluntary organisation, Ebong Alap.

Sayantan Dasgupta teaches Comparative Literature in Jadavpur University and is also the co-ordinator of the Centre for Translation in Indian Literatures (Centil) at JU.

Somak Ghoshal is commissioning editor, literary fiction, Penguin India. He writes on literature, the fine arts, music and politics, and translates between English and Bengali.

Sutanuka Ghosh is assistant professor in the department of English, Jadavpur University.

Vikram Iyengar is a Kathak dancer and artistic director of Ranan, a performance collective.